Hans-Peter Zimmermann

How to Heal
Your Inner Family

A New Approach to Family Constellation Work
for Lay People and Professionals

Bibliographic Information published by the German National Library
The German National Library lists this publication in the German Nation Bibliography.
Detailed bibliographical data are available on the Internet via portal.d-nb.de.

Manufacturer and Publisher:
Books on Demand GmbH, D-22848 Norderstedt, Germany (www.bod.de)
ISBN 9783732242351

1st Edition (German) 2010
2nd Edition (German) 2010
3rd Edition (German) 2013

1st Edition in English 2013

Editor of English Version:
Laurie Lamson

Illustrations:
Anita Zimmermann

Original title (German):
„Ich achte dein Schicksal – sechs systemische Checks für Hypnotherapeuten"
Translated by Trusted Translations Inc. www.trustedtranslations.com

Content

Who Is This Book For?

Dear readers,

This book is interesting for three target groups:

- Therapists and coaches with systemic experience
- Therapists and coaches without systemic experience
- Lay people

This book will give therapists with systemic experience step-by-step instructions on how they can apply their knowledge in a one-on-one setting. They will also learn an efficient method that allows them to do a kind of systemic "spring cleaning" on their clients.

Therapists with no systemic experience will realize how valuable this therapeutic tool is after reading this book. And they will most likely look for a good systemic instructor.

The lay person will find out what they can expect from systemic therapy. It is anticipated: This is a lot of information, and it might actually mean a breakthrough for you in your life. I've even made "old hands" cry and subsequently beam with joy with these techniques...

Regardless of how hard your fate may be: I honor it by leaving it with you. And that includes the fate of having bought this book ;-)

Gstaad/Switzerland, August 2013

Hans-Peter Zimmermann

How Were the Six Systemic Checks Developed?

Maybe you even wonder, when reading my biography, over the fact that my previous books have dealt mainly with economic topics. Therefore, I will briefly tell you about my therapeutic career.

After high school and six semesters of language study to become a teacher, I was fed up with the academic environment and became a real man-of-action and self-made man. Do not ask me why; probably my wife, with whom I've been since 1980, woke me up. I held jobs in the film and video industry, and as an international sales manager for film audio-dubbing equipment and, on the side, helped my wife make her weight-loss clinic in Berne into a gold mine.

In 1986 I started my own business, first as an advertising consultant for small businesses. Due to my quick success, my activities increasingly expanded to areas of management consulting.

In 1991 I recorded my experiences in my first book, "Great Success in Small Business," that today, even after 19 years, still sells like hotcakes. In 1989, I began to hold "slightly different" sales seminars; later advertising and time management seminars were added, and soon there were about six different seminars on personal development topics, success training and marketing small businesses.

In 1992 my wife and I decided to rent a vacation home in San Clemente near Los Angeles and fly to Switzerland to hold seminars several times a year. I learned to fly helicopters and took an independent postgraduate course in Clinical Hypnosis. If you are interested, you can download my doctoral papers, which comprise something more than a thousand pages, at www.hpz.com/hypnosis-doctoral-papers.

During this training, I learned, among other things, about Timeline Therapy according to Tad James and it was an incredible discovery for me. For the first time I had a tool in my hand with which I could easily neutralize negative emotions triggered by certain events in my past. In time, I realized that the original Timeline Therapy achieved an even more lasting impact when it was combined with classical regression therapy and elements of psychodrama.

However, certain areas of my psyche and the psyches of my clients seemed unreachable... until I discovered systemic work in 2003.

I must shamefully admit that the first systemic years were marked by just muddling through and frequent lucky breaks. In other words, I often knew that I had done something right, but was completely in the dark as to how it happened.

But the universe, as you know, doesn't do things halfway. The heavens rushed to my assistance with a massive crisis and as a result (surely you are aware that there is an opportunity in every crisis), I learned how to always know what I'm doing with systemic work.

Eventually it occurred to me that I always took the same therapeutic steps when I only had two hours available for a client, and that these steps made the clients incredibly strong. I had found my most effective form of therapy. Then I began to analyze the steps and realized that I hadn't read about this sequence anywhere: Thus, the six Systemic Checks for Hypnotherapists were born!

Now I just have to write them down, so that you, too, can benefit from them.

Gstaad/Switzerland, August 2013

Hans-Peter Zimmermann

Systemic Check No. 1: Exterior View of the Family of Origin

The first thing I always do is to help my clients understand how their family of origin came into being. This is not a treatment step, merely an inventory. However, it often has a therapeutic effect in that the client understands how the family emerged, how the individual members responded to the arrival of a new family member, and the situation into which he or she was born. As our first fictional example, let's take a look at a 35-year-old man named Markus who grew up with his parents and reported no unusual events in his family of origin.

Example 1

Therapist:
Did you grow up normally with your parents?

Client:
Yes.

Therapist:
Are your parents still alive?

Client:
Yes.

Therapist:
And they're still together?

Client:
Yes.

Therapist:
What are your parents' first names?

Client:
Martin and Elsbeth.

Therapist:
What's the oldest child's name?

Client:
That would be me.

Therapist:
Do you have brothers and sisters?

Client:
Yes, a sister and a brother.

Therapist:
Your sister is the second oldest?

Client:
Yes.

Therapist:
What's her name?

Client:
Teresa.

Therapist:
And your little brother?

Client:
Bernard.

Therapist:
Do you know if your mother had any miscarriages or abortions?

Client:
No, not that I know of.

Therapist:
Good. Please lie down, close your eyes and imagine that we are in a big market square. In this square, there is a large clock on the ground with a large face about thirty feet in diameter.
And now let's put your family of origin on this dial. We'll start with your parents at the time when they were already

together, but didn't have any children yet. Where would we put Martin? Close to what number?

Client:
On the twelve.

Therapist:
Directly on the twelve, or a little toward the center?

Client:
A little toward the center.

Therapist:
About how much?

Client:
About a third of the way from the edge.

Therapist:
And in what direction is he looking?

Client:
Downwards.

Therapist:
What does that mean? In the direction of what number?

Client:
Toward the six.

Therapist:
Good, then let's add Elsbeth at the time when she was already with Martin but didn't have any children yet. Where do we put her?

Client:
On the five.

Therapist:
Directly on the five or a little toward the center?

Client:
Directly on the edge of the clock.

Therapist:
And in what direction is she looking?

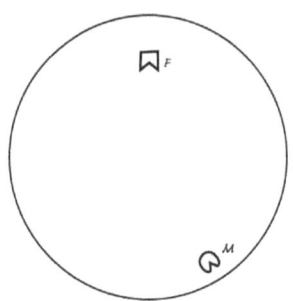

Client:
On the five

Therapist:
You mean outside of the clock?

Client:
Yes.

Therapist:
Good, imagine you could slip into the role of Martin. If he looks slightly over to the left, he sees his wife Elsbeth's back about 27 feet away. How is Martin doing with his Elsbeth?

Client:
Yes, he is asking himself why she's not looking at him.

Therapist:
And how does he feel?

Client:
Kind of sad, and he doesn't understand.

Therapist:
Good, now imagine you could slip into the role of Elsbeth. She feels her husband Martin about 27 feet behind her. How is she doing with her Martin?

Client:
She'd like to leave, but is afraid.

Therapist:
Can you see why she is afraid?

Client:
Her parents want her to marry Martin. They think he's a good match.

Therapist:
Now Markus is born. Where do we put him?

I talk about the client intentionally in the third person, because I want him to initially see the family as a neutral observer. It is also easier that way for him to jump from role to role.

Incidentally, most clients can empathize amazingly well with each role. Very rarely does someone say they don't know how each person felt. Whether their lack of empathy is due to strong defense mechanisms or a lack of emotional and social intelligence, I can't tell. There is certainly still room for more research.

In such cases, I switch to my extensive range of tools for therapy resistance, which I don't want to go into here because it is beyond the scope of this book.

Client:
Let's put him to the left of his mother.

Therapist:
What is left? More toward the four or more in the direction of the six?

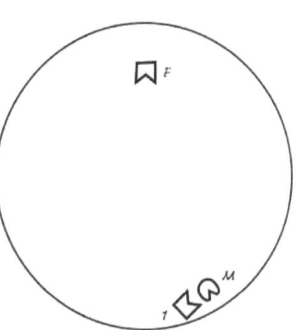

Client:
More toward the six.

Therapist:
And what direction is he looking in?

Client:
At his mother.

Therapist:
That means Markus is looking at his mother from the side?

Client:
Exactly.

At this point the experienced therapist will already foresee certain issues that will need to be cleared up later. Firstly, there is the Oedipus issue in the broadest sense. That is, the son feels that the mother is "alone" and unconsciously he wants to either replace the partner or believes that the mother expects him to replace the partner. Secondly, when a child stands laterally to a parent, this position often means that the child wants to prevent the parent from leaving. In this case, both seem to be true, which is congruent with the optical position.

> Therapist:
> And how does Markus feel?
>
> Client:
> Not so good.
>
> Therapist:
> What does that mean?
>
> Client:
> Somehow cold. No one really notices me.
>
> Therapist:
> How's Elsbeth now that she has a son?
>
> Client:
> Ambivalent.
>
> Therapist:
> Ambivalent to what extent?
>
> Client:
> On the one hand she's happy that I'm there. On the other hand, it binds her now to her husband.
>
> Therapist:
> And how is Martin with his son?
>
> Client:
> Actually good. He is proud. And he hopes his wife will pay more attention to him now.
>
> Therapist:
> And? Does she?
>
> Client:
> No, she's almost a little defiant. As if she wants to say: "Now I have my son."

Therapist:
Good, then Teresa is born. Where do we put her?

Client:
With the father.

Therapist:
Where exactly?

Client:
To his left.

Therapist:
So, toward one o'clock?

Client:
No, I was just looking at the clock from above. More toward eleven o'clock.

Here it becomes clear how important it is to always use the numbers on the clock for orientation. "Left" can have different meanings, depending on how you look at it. Therefore, the therapist should always ask, "Close to what number". The clock's face is used as an orientation guide. Of course, it would be possible to let the client open their eyes and ask them to plot the positions themselves, but that would make the trance work impossible, or at least, very difficult.

Therapist:
Is Teresa at the same level as the father or is she more toward the edge or center of the clock?

Client:
At the same level.

Therapist:
And what direction is he looking in?

Client:
In the same direction as the father.

Therapist:
So, in the direction of six o'clock?

Client:
Yes.

Therapist:
And how's Teresa?

Client:
Not so good.

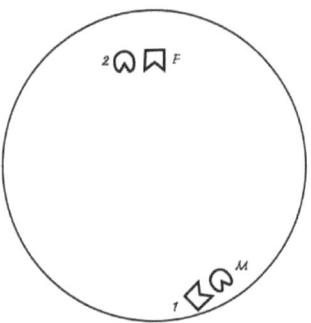

Therapist:
Can you elaborate?

Client:
She doesn't really know where she belongs. And her mother is too far away.

Therapist:
And how is Markus with his sister?

Client:
It'd actually be really nice to have a sister. But somehow she's too far away from me. And now I'm not getting enough attention from Dad.

Therapist:
How's Elsbeth now that she has a daughter?

Client:
She is a little overwhelmed. Now, with two children, there is no escape. And it's a bit much for her.

Therapist:
How's Martin now that he has a daughter?

Client:
Actually quite good. He is proud. And he's glad he's not so alone anymore. But he'd rather have his wife by his side.

Therapist:
Now Bernard is born. Where do we put him?

Client:
He's on the three.

Therapist:
At the edge of the clock or a little toward the center?

Client:
Right on the edge.

Therapist:
And what direction is he looking in?

Client:
Toward nine o'clock.

Therapist:
And how's Bernard?

Client:
He doesn't quite know what he's doing here. To the left are two people spending time together and to the right over there, too. Somehow that's not really a family.

Therapist:
How's Teresa with her younger brother?

Client:
She barely notices him.

Therapist:
How's Markus with his younger brother?

Client:
He thinks it's quite exciting. And he doesn't have to focus so much on his mother.

Therapist:
How's Elsbeth with her second son?

Client:
Now it's definitely too much for her. She wants to get away.

Therapist:
How's Martin with his second son?

Client:
Actually good. But now he fears that he's going to lose his wife because he sees how overwhelmed she is.

That is the first Systemic Check. The therapist's notepad looks something like this:

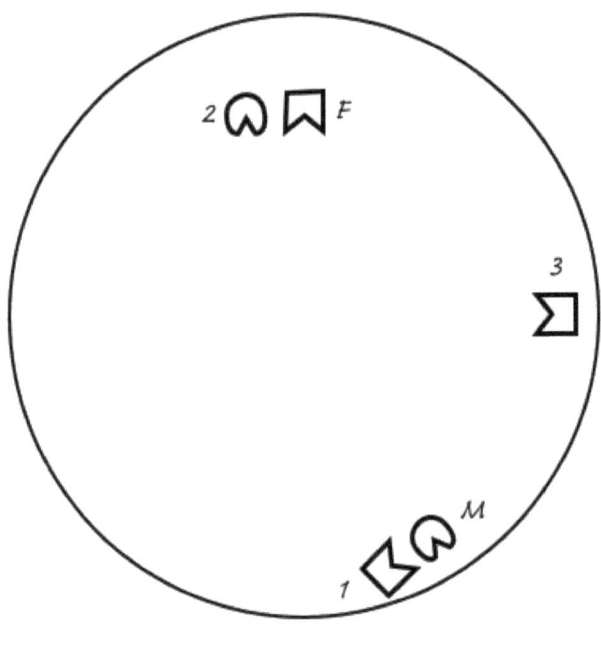

Martin F
Elsbeth M
Markus 1
Teresa 2
Bernard 3

The squares indicate males and circles indicate females. The notch indicates in what direction the person is looking. "M" stands for mother; "F" stands for father. The numbers indicate the birth order of the children.

It is important that you make it clear to the client from the outset (if necessary by repeating it several times) how large the diameter of the clock is, namely thirty feet. Only then can he symbolically represent the distance that may reign in his family.

Summary Check No. 1

- Where does each family member go? In what direction is each one looking?

- How does each family member feel?

- Gradually build the family without clarifying anything!

Systemic Check No. 2: The Masculine and the Feminine Powerhouse

The second Systemic Check consists of two parts. Systemic Check 2a is the strength of the male line, Systemic Check 2b is the strength of the female line. What does this mean?

a) The Masculine Powerhouse

When a person is disoriented, doesn't feel his roots, suffers from a lack of self-confidence, can't "stand his ground" (this also applies to women), doesn't stick to his values, doesn't enjoy his success, you can almost bet that there's a break in the male ancestral line. I've also found a broken male line in every case of drug addiction. To help you better understand what this means, here are a few examples of broken male lines:

- The client's father (F) died early. Whereby "early" always means that the client was a child, usually younger than 16 years. Although deaths of parents in later years are also bad, they do not have the same effect systemically as an earlier death.

- The client had not known his father, because he left the mother around the time of the birth, for example, or because the client is the result of an affair.
  Of course, very bad fates are observed when the client is the result of rape. I will introduce healing approaches for these cases later.
  A complicating factor is if the father is a taboo subject; he is not talked about because he hurt the mother so much. Thereby, half of the client is denied, biologically speaking.

- From my experience, if something similar happened with one of the client's ancestors, for example, if the father (F) lost his father (FF) early or did not know him, it has the same effect on the male energy. If a stepfather's name is taken, this has an additional debilitating effect on many clients.

- Also systemically important are the fates of displaced people (Silesia, Sudetenland, Pomerania, etc.), regardless of in which generation the displacement occurred.

- In about 90 percent of all cases, discovering their true origin (country) is of paramount importance. For example, if the great-grandfather immigrated from Italy to Germany, it is highly relevant systemically. I'll illustrate how to deal with this issue and how to solve the problem of the homeless by using examples of therapy.

  Incidentally, in this systemic observation lies a great deal of healing potential for American souls, since many of them have foreign ancestors. It's one thing to be proud of the nation that received you well; it's another thing to give your real home a place in your heart.

Example 2

Therapist:

Imagine that your father is standing behind you. Behind him is his father, your grandfather. Behind him is his father, your great-grandfather, behind him is his father, your great-great grandfather. And behind him is his father, your great-great-great grandfather. And each one puts his hands on the shoulders of his son. You feel your father's hands on your shoulders. Feel for a moment what it feels like when the energy of five male ancestors flows to you.

Various reactions are possible here, for example:

- It feels good, but could be more.

- (In cases where the ancestors suffered traumatic fates) It's very oppressive and is so heavy that it pushes me into the ground. I would prefer to get out of here.

So you can imagine what kind of internal image the client has, here is a drawing that my wife Anita made:

For female clients it looks like this:

Now it is time to repair this masculine powerhouse step by step. There is no recommended order. It is important however, that the therapist is always aware of what he wants to achieve, namely, that the energy can flow freely from the great-great-great-grandfather to the client. The individuals in this line must be treated only as far back as is necessary, in order to allow the energy to flow.

If you are wondering how the client could know what happened to his forefathers, I can reassure you: That's the beauty of trance work. In this state your client sees spontaneous internal images and knows everything. Only in very rare cases of extreme dissociation have I seen a client who is absolutely unable to do trance work.

Incidentally, there are systemic therapists who require extensive genealogical research from their clients before working with them. This can be useful in order to get to a problem quicker. However, in some cases, there is simply nothing known about the ancestors. Then you have to depend on these mental images that are spontaneously supplied by the client.

I've also seen cases where genealogical research was actually a hindrance. Or how do you find out through genealogical research that your great-grandfather was fathered by a German servant, and therefore was not Swiss, but German? In other words: With genealogical research, you definitely cannot discover the numerous cases of cowbird eggs!

Before I burden you with more theory, let's continue with an example:

Example 3

Therapist:
How does it feel to have five generations of male ancestors behind you?

Client:
Okay.

Therapist:
Turn around and say, "Hi, Dad" to your father. Say it out loud.

Client:
Hi, Dad.

Therapist:
How does that make you feel?

Client:
Yeah, somehow distant.

Therapist:
Was there something missing with your father? Do you wish you'd had more love; more attention from him?

Client:
Yes.

Therapist:
Then say to him, "Dad, I wish I'd had a little more love and attention from you."

Client:
Dad, I wish I'd had a little more love and attention from you.

Therapist:
How does your father feel when he hears that?

Client:
He's at a bit of a loss. And also sad.

Therapist:
Then slip into the role of your father, and he says to his son:
"My son, I would have gladly given you more, but I couldn't."

Client:
My son, I would have gladly given you more, but I couldn't.

Therapist:
How does that make the son feel?

Perhaps you've noticed that I often speak to clients in the third person during role play. I don't want the client to identify with any particular role, but rather that he be able to switch at the touch of a button from one role to the next. This has at least two advantages. First, it gets the client a little bit out of the role of the victim, and secondly, he understands the systemic connections better.

Client:
It is a little bit easier.

Therapist:
Slip into the role of the son and say to his father: "Dad, I got the most important thing from you. My life. And for that I thank you. The rest I'll do myself."

If you know that your client struggles with his fate, then the sentence "I thank you" is not a good idea. In that case, you would have to have him say for example "I'm still having a little trouble accepting this gift from you, but I'm in the process of learning how."

Client:
Dad, I got the most important thing from you. My life. And for that I thank you. The rest I'll do myself.

Therapist:
And how does that feel?

Client:
(Sighs, relieved) Very good.

Therapist:
How does the father feel?

Client:
He's now standing taller.

Therapist:
Stay in the role of the son and tell your father, "Dad, everything I've carried for you, I'm giving back to you now. It's better off with you. I am only the child. And I'm going to go play now."

Client:
Dad, everything I've carried for you, I'm giving back to you now. It's better off with you. I am only the child. And I'm going to go play now.

Therapist:
How does that feel?

Client:
It's getting easier. But I'm still afraid of giving everything back to him. He has a lot to bear himself.

Therapist:
Then slip into the role of your father. He turns to his father and says, "Hi, Dad".

Client:
Hi, Dad.

Therapist:
How does your father feel?

Client:
Stressed.

Therapist:
What does that mean?

It is very important that the therapist always understands what the client means. In linguistics, it is said that language has a surface structure and a deep structure. The surface structure is the words that we use, and the deep structure is the meaning we attach to these words. If one word has several meanings, the therapist must identify what meaning it has for the client. In Neurolinguistic Programming (NLP) this process is called "chunking down".

Client:
He feels sorry for his dad. He is also quite small.

In systemic therapy this is called a "presumption" or "parentification". The child puts himself above a parent, making himself feel somewhat bigger. At the same time, this also means that the child is burdened with the fate of the parent. Because it's just logical that the bigger one bears the burden for the smaller one. But this is wrong systemically and leads to problems for everyone involved.

Therapist:
Do you know anything about your grandfather, that is your father's father?

In this example, the client actually knows something. But even if this weren't the case, you could use a technique that I will describe later to find out what happened that was of importance.

Client:
Yes, my grandparents were expelled from Silesia.

Therapist:
Then stay in the role of your father and he says to his father: "Dad, you and Mom, you were expelled from Silesia. And that was bad. "

Client:
Dad, you and Mom, you were expelled from Silesia. And that
was bad.

Therapist:
Is that true? Was it bad?

It is crucial that such sentences are always verified for their accuracy, for
example, with questions such as "Does that feel right". Because if something doesn't feel right for the client and the therapist just ignores it, it
would eventually lead to a break in the rapport. If you observe the client
closely, you can usually see whether a sentence is true or not.

Client:
Yes, it was bad.

Therapist:
Then your father should say to his father: "Dad, you were
mad at Silesia, because you think Silesia drove you into exile."

Client:
Dad, you were mad at Silesia, because you think Silesia drove
you into exile.

Therapist:
Is that true? Was he angry?

Client:
Yes, he's totally pissed.

Therapist:
Then your father should say to him: "But it's not Silesia's
fault. It was the people who ruled Silesia. Silesia is our home.
Our roots are in Silesia. And Silesia will always have a place in
my heart."

This is called a Reframe in linguistics. The loaded word "Silesia" gets a
new meaning. The negative feelings that were previously associated with

it are now blamed on the responsible politicians. Thus, the word "Silesia" becomes a symbol of home and belonging.

Incidentally, in this case, you have to define not the country but the region as the homeland, just like you do for the Sudetenland, Alsace, or South Tyrol for example, because these regions have belonged to different nations over the years.

The problem of "being angry at a country" can also occur in the case of Germany, for example, because of the country's Nazi past. In this case it is also important to separate the country from the responsible people ("It's not Germany's fault; it was the people who then governed Germany") so that Germany (not political Germany, but the land) can be accepted as the home.

Further, a client may condemn a country of origin because his father, who comes from there, has hurt him very deeply. In this case it is also necessary to separate the country from the people ("Dad, you've hurt me greatly and because you're Italian, I've condemned Italy. Now I see that Italy has nothing to do with it. Italy is my home, that's where my roots are, and I'm proud to be Italian.")

When you are systemically trained, try it out. You will be amazed what miracles you can work with this therapeutic tool!

Client:
But it's not Silesia's fault. It was the people who ruled Silesia. Silesia is our home. Our roots are in Silesia. And Silesia will always have a place in my heart.

Therapist:
What does it do to your grandfather?

Client:
(*His facial expression shows that there are massive changes taking place*) He starts to cry.

Therapist:
Are those tears of sorrow or tears of joy?

Client:
(In tears) Joy.

Therapist:
Slip into the role of your grandfather, and he says to his son: "I can finally feel my roots again. And you can feel them too."

Client:
I can finally feel my roots again. And you can feel them too.

Therapist:
How's that for your father and grandfather?

Client:
They've both gotten bigger. And it's really like they've grown roots.

Therapist:
Slip again in the role of your father, and he says to his father: "Look Dad, this is my son, Markus, who I had with Elsbeth. Things have continued well."

Client:
Look Dad, this is my son, Markus, who I had with Elsbeth. Things have continued well.

Therapist:
How does your father feel?

Client:
Super. He's very proud of me.

Therapist:
And how do you feel?

Client:
Sensational!

Therapist:
Are you ready to go play now?

Client:
(Enthusiastically) Yes!

Therapist:
Good. Imagine you're an engineer and had to check this masculine powerhouse. Look at these five male ancestors. Is the connection between you and your father intact? Can the energy flow to you from your father?

Client:
(Spontaneously) Yes.

Therapist:
And from your grandfather to your father?

Client:
(Spontaneously) Yes.

Therapist:
From great-grandfather to grandfather?

Client:
(Spontaneously) Yes.

Therapist:
From great-great-grandfather to the great-grandfather?

Client:
(Hesitates) Hmmm ...

Therapist:
Not quite so apparent yet. Slip into the role of your great-grandfather. He turns to his father and says, "Hi. Dad".

Client:
Hi, Dad.

Therapist:
What does your great-grandfather feel?

Client:
Nothing. There's nothing there.

Therapist:
What do you mean, there's nothing there?

Client:
I can't see anyone.

Please note that the client has never previously claimed to not be able to see anyone. Doing so now is of specific significance and should be explored to find out why. And I'll tell you again: You do not need to do any genealogical research. The client's mental pictures and the probing sentences fully suffice to restore the energy flow with the help of the necessary measures.

> Therapist:
> Then say: "Dad, I can't see you."
>
> Client:
> Dad, I can't see you.
>
> Therapist:
> You left too soon.
>
> Client:
> You left too soon.
>
> Therapist:
> Does that feel right?
>
> Client:
> No.

What reasons could there be for him not being able to see his father? He could have died when the son was still very young. This is clearly not the case here, as can be deduced from the client's spontaneous, "No". Thus, further exploration is needed.

> Therapist:
> Say the sentence: "I never knew you."
>
> Client:
> (Clearly has trouble saying the sentence) I never knew you.
> (Starts to cry)

You'll be surprised how unerringly your clients know what is true and what is not under hypnosis and, most importantly, how they react to it emotionally, even though it concerns an ancestor and not the client himself.

Therapist:
That seems to be true, right?

Client:
(Still crying) Yes.

Therapist:
Then say: "I have a right to know my father. I want to see you now."

Client:
I have a right to know my father. I want to see you now.

Therapist:
Can you see him now?

Client:
(Crying even harder, but happy) Yes.

Therapist:
Then say: "You're finally here, Dad."

Client:
You're finally here, Dad.

You might also be forced at this point to call on the mother to clarify certain aspects. But you should not lose sight of the focus being on the male line.

Therapist:
Imagine, the great-grandfather's mother is standing in front of him. You stay in your role and say to her: "Mom, you deprived me of my father."

Client:
Mom, you deprived me of my father.

Therapist:
How does the mother react?

Client:
She is embarrassed.

Therapist:
Then tell her, "Mom, I have a right to know who my father is, because I am made up of half from you and half out of him."

Client:
Mom, I have a right to know who my father is, because I am made up of half from you and half out of him.

Therapist:
How does the great-grandfather's mother react?

Client:
Coolly, she's aloof.

In this case, I use a helpful therapy tool I call cathartic role play. You'll notice the difference to the systemic role play immediately:

Therapist:
Imagine that I could talk to this great-great-grandmother and I said, "Hey, what's gotten into you, not to tell your son who his father is?! Do you know what you are doing to him?" What would she say if she could talk?

Client:
(In the role of the great-great-grandmother:) That's none of your business.

Therapist:
(With emphasis:) Oh, but it is my business! Your great-great-grandson is here with me on the treatment couch because you were too cowardly to admit your affair. How many generations have to suffer until you realize that?

Client:
(In the role the great-great-grandmother, much softer:) I didn't know that it is so bad.

Therapist:
Now you know. Please tell your son, "My dear son, I didn't know that not knowing your father was so bad for you."

You'll have noticed that we've now returned to systemic role play.

> Client:
> My dear son, I didn't know that not knowing your father was so bad for you.
>
> Therapist:
> I was ashamed because it was an affair and I didn't want to jeopardize the family. You were too important to me.
>
> Client:
> I was ashamed because it was an affair and I didn't want to jeopardize the family. You were too important to me.
>
> Therapist:
> Does that feel right?
>
> Client:
> Yes. And now my great-grandfather isn't mad at her anymore, because she wanted to save the family.
>
> Therapist:
> Stay in her role and say, "You can now have him as your father, and he will always be your father."
>
> Client:
> You can now have him as your father, and he will always be your father.
>
> Therapist:
> And I also respect him in you.
>
> Client:
> And I also respect him in you.
>
> Therapist:
> Good, the great-great-grandmother can go. Does the energy now flow from your great-great-grandfather to your great-grandfather?
>
> Client:
> Yes.

Please note: The interlude with the great-great-grandmother was only necessary because otherwise it probably would not have been possible to "repair" the connection between the great-great-grandfather and the great-grandfather. Of course there were numerous conflicts between the individual ancestors that could be treated. But ultimately this is about our client and we only have to do what is necessary for him to be able to feel his roots really well.

Therapist:
And if I asked your great-great grandfather, "Are you also Silesian?" What would he say?

Client:
Yes.

Therapist:
How is the connection between great-great-great-grandfather and great-great-grandfather, in other words, from the rearmost in the line to his son?

Client:
It's good.

Therapist:
And is he also Silesian?

Client:
Yes.

Therapist:
Good. Then stand in front of your father again with your back to him. Each of your five male ancestors has his hands on the shoulders of his son. You feel your father's hands on your shoulders. And feel what has changed.

Client:
(Obviously changed) Ah, that's powerful!

Therapist:
Yes, let the energy flow. Let it really recharge your batteries.

Feel how the masculine energy comes in through your shoulders and flows down to your feet, and even further into the ground. And you stand there like a tree.

Client:
It feels sensational!

I would like to introduce you to three "turbos" that make this energy flow even more. By the way, please don't underestimate the effect of this intervention! I know many entrepreneurs for whom success really took off after this. And of course, it is also extremely productive for a couple's relationship when the man is completely connected to his masculine energy and the wife to her feminine energy.

The first turbo was not my idea. It's been around since there have been family constellations.

Therapist:
Turn around again and say to these men: "We men."

Client:
We men.

Therapist:
How does that feel?

Client:
Super. They've all gotten bigger.

Turbo number two was half my idea. I have derived it from the fact that for ninety percent of people, acknowledging their country of origin is vital when it comes to feeling their roots. And especially in cases where the homeland was "demonized", you can accomplish a lot if you use this turbo.

Therapist:
Say to your male ancestors: "We Silesians".

Client:
We Silesians.

Therapist:
How does that feel?

Client:
I'm almost bursting with self-confidence.

Turbo Number three is, I believe, my own invention. And it goes like this:

Therapist:
Take a good look at these men. Does one of them come across as particularly strong, especially masculine?

Client:
The second from the back.

Therapist:
Good, then go up to him and say, "great-great grandfather, I could use some more of your masculine energy."

Client:
Great-great grandfather, I could use some more of your masculine energy.

Therapist:
Then slip into the role of the great-great grandfather and say, "I give it to my child, he to his, and so on, until it gets to you."

Client:
I give it to my child, he to his, and so on, until it gets to you.

Therapist:
Now stand with your back to your father again and feel if anything has changed.

Client:
Yes, the energy flows more intensely.

A systemic therapist once criticized this step by saying: "You're making the client dependent on whether the ancestor wants to give this energy or not."

In my experience, however, the ancestors are always willing to pass on this energy, provided that the therapist has previously done everything right. The problem usually lies not with the giver, but with the receiver. And with the words, "I could use a little more of your energy", the client is only expressing his willingness to receive what his ancestors want to give him.

Please understand me correctly: This does not mean that the descendant demands more than the gift of life from his ancestors; that would be neurotic. With this ritual, we are primarily causing the descendant to receive his life and connect with his ancestors.

> Therapist:
> Good. Recharge your batteries with this masculine energy as long as you want. And you know that you can conjure this image of your male ancestors again any time you need it. It will help you when it comes to your self-confidence, when it comes to "standing your ground" in your career, to be aware of your worth and to demand enough money, and, of course, when you are with your wife, because what is more wonderful than a man who can be all man, when he is with a woman who can be all woman.

For a female client, you would adjust the last sentence accordingly, of course. The rest, however, is also carried out exactly the same way in terms of the Fatherland. Before you damn me as patriarch, just let me say: Don't take my word for it; try it out! For example, if a client's mother is French and the father is German, have your client (well-understood after the masculine and feminine powerhouse have been repaired) try the following sentences:

"I am French" and "I am German." In most cases, the origin of the father will have more energy for the clients.

b) The Feminine Powerhouse

If a person cannot show love, lacks warmth and cannot deal with his feelings, then usually the female line is broken somewhere. You can proceed in exactly the same way as with the male line, with the following exceptions:

- The roots are determined by the male line. However, if the client's mother doesn't feel her roots, it may be useful to identify her roots. This is done exactly as I've shown you in the male line, i.e. with the client's internal images. This background is then only for the mother. The daughter's origin stems from her father's roots.
- If in the female line, the energy doesn't flow from a mother to her daughter, in addition to all the procedures you now know from the male line, you can try the following phrases:
    - "In my family, the men were not respected."
    - "In my family, the women were not respected."
    - "Being a woman is dangerous."

"Trying" means always having the client say the sentence out loud and asking whether if feels true. I will give you another example shortly.

- There are some women who misunderstand the term "strong woman". They think they are strong women, because they have or display a lot of male energy. This is of course allowed, and is even a must in our business life. You can't get by without male energy in business. However, such a business woman is not a "strong woman" but a woman with a strong masculine energy. A strong woman is a woman with strong feminine energy. Many women who have considered themselves to be strong are very surprised when they allow this feminine energy to flow for the first time. It is described by most as "warm," "soft" or "round". And it has a lot to do with abandonment. What I always tell these women is: "You don't need to be afraid of losing the masculine energy because of this. You still have it abundantly available. Now you just have something extra available to you."

- Through experimentation, I have found that it's better for the feminine energy to enter via the hips and then radiate up and down through the body. So I explain to clients that the woman behind them is touching the hips of her child:

A practical example may help you visualize the work with the female line:

Example 4

Therapist:
Imagine your mother is standing behind you, behind her is her mother, your grandmother, behind her is your great-grandmother, behind her is your great-great-grandmother, and behind her is your great-great-great-grandmother. Five generations of female ancestors and the women have their hands on the hips of their child.
So you feel your mother's hands on your hips.
Take a moment to feel what it's like to have five generations of female ancestors standing behind you.

Client:
Weak.

Therapist:
What does that mean?

Client:
There is almost nothing there. I feel there are expectations of me that I can't fulfill.

A principle in systemic work is: "The energy flows from the parents to the children. The child doesn't have to give anything back. If he or she wants to give something back then he should give it to his children or to an equivalent child substitute."
Unfortunately, people keep trying to turn this energy flow around. A mother wants to be "fed" by her daughter or a son acts as his mother's "protector". If you are systemically trained, you know what I mean.

Therapist:
Then turn around to your mother and say, "Hi, Mom".

Client:
Hi, Mom.

Therapist:

How does that feel?

Client:
Distant.

Therapist:
Does that mean you would have liked to have been closer to her?

Client:
No.

Therapist:
You didn't want to be closer to your mother?

Client:
She couldn't give more.

You can tell that this client is systemically trained. He has obviously already heard the phrase "I would have liked to have given you more, but I couldn't." Of course, you can't leave it at that because this answer doesn't come from the heart, but from the intellect. A reframe is suggested:

Therapist:
I'll be honest with you. I've never seen a child who would have liked a distant relationship with his mother.

Client:
No, of course I would have liked to be closer to her. But I also realize that she couldn't give any more than she did.

Therapist:
Did you realize this as a small child?

Client:
No.

Therapist:
Okay, then slip into the role of your inner child and say, "Mom, I would have liked a little more closeness and warmth

from you."

Client:
Mom, I would have liked a little more closeness and warmth from you.

Therapist:
What does it do to your mother?

Client:
She says: "I didn't get any more either."

You have probably already guessed what needs to be done now, right? Correct, that cries out for a confrontation between the mother and grandmother:

Therapist:
Then slip into the role of your mother who turns to her mother and says, "Hi, Mom".

Client:
Hi mom.

Therapist:
How does your mother feel?

Client:
Also distant.

Therapist:
What can you tell me about your mother's childhood?

This question is usually answered in the introductory conversation, of course. I just wanted to illustrate that it is not a disaster if you suddenly think that you have forgotten something while taking the client's history, you can always make up for it during the therapy session.

Client:
She was the eldest of eight children. Her mother worked and

was in the store all day. My mother had to look after her younger siblings.

Therapist:
And do you know if she liked doing that?

Client:
No.

Therapist:
No, you don't know? Or no, she didn't like doing it?

Client:
She hated it. She later told me that when she had her own children, her first thought was, "Here we go again."

Therapist:
Then stay in the role of your mother and say to her mother: "Mom, I had to work early. Too early. I would have rather played. "

Client:
(Obviously fighting back tears)

As a good therapist, I hope you know how important it is that the client trusts himself to abreact. So please never lapse into "Kleenexitis", as I've seen with some therapists. "Kleenexitis" is the tendency of therapists to nip any abreaction in the bud by holding a Kleenex box under the client's nose. This is approximately equivalent to the suggestion: "Stop crying, I can't stand it."

This response by a therapist is counterproductive and should really be avoided. Many problems are caused precisely by the fact that their mourning process wasn't completed. Forget about the make-up that could smear with female clients. These are more important things at the moment! A good therapist will therefore encourage the client to cry. Like this, for example:

Therapist:
Yes, if something comes up that you don't need any more, just let it out. This is a safe place and now is the right time

for it. It's been held back long enough; it's caused you enough problems. Let your mother's tears out.

The last sentence is a good trick to weaken the self-control of certain clients a bit. At the beginning of therapy, it's easier for many clients to pretend that they are crying their mother's tears instead of their own.

> Therapist:
> Stay in the role of your mother and she says to her mother, "Mom, I had to work early. Too early. I would have rather played."
>
> Client:
> Mom, I had to work early. Too early. I would rather have played. *(Strong abreaction)*
>
> Therapist:
> How does your grandmother feel about that?
>
> Client:
> She is completely perplexed. She didn't expect that. She's also fighting back tears.
>
> Therapist:
> Slip into the role of your grandmother and she says to her daughter: "Dear child, we had to support you and your seven siblings, Dad and I."
>
> Client:
> Dear child, we had to support you and your seven siblings, Dad and I.
>
> Therapist:
> It wasn't easy but we did it.
>
> Client:
> It wasn't easy but we did it.
>
> Therapist:
> I'm sorry that we couldn't give you more emotional warmth.

Client:
I'm sorry that we couldn't give you more emotional warmth.

Therapist:
Everything that you carried for us parents, we're taking it back now. It's better off with us.

Client:
Everything that you carried for us parents, we're taking it back now. It's better off with us.

Therapist:
You're just a child. And you can go play now.

Client:
You're just a child. And you can go play now.

These sentences often cause the client to cry tears of liberation and you can tell that a heavy burden has been lifted. In this case, the client has also felt why his mother couldn't give more than she gave. There's really a huge difference between someone simply "realizing" something intellectually and experiencing it emotionally.

When the mother (in the role of the child) is afraid to "go play" at this point, you have to find out why. Reasons for this may include:

- The child feels that his mother isn't being supported by her husband be it because he is not present physically (death, divorce, etc.) or because he is emotionally absent. That means that the child thinks he has to fill the gap left by the partner. This is also called an attenuated Oedipus or Electra issue. In this case resolving sentences include: "Mom, the place next to you was empty and I thought about taking it. But it's not mine. I am only the child. What happened between you and Dad is none of my business. You must have been compatible in some way, you and Dad. You gave me life. The rest I'll do myself. "

- The child feels that his mother is trying to help carry the fate of his parents. In such cases, there's a sentence that I myself developed that has proven to be valuable, "Mom, if you're carrying something for your parents, please give it back to them. Because everyone is responsible for handling his own destiny. But only his own." This sentence often causes the whole ancestral line to only carry its own burden in one fell swoop.

To conclude this chapter, I would like to give you a few examples of special cases:

Example 5: Roots in the Case of Gypsies

Therapist:
If I asked your father, "Are you German?" What would he say? "

Client:
(spontaneously) Yes.

Therapist:
If I were to ask your grandfather, "Are you German?" What would he say?

Client:
(spontaneously) Yes.

Therapist:
If I were to ask your great-grandfather, "Are you German?" What would he say?

Client:
(Silent, his expression shows rejection)

Therapist:
It doesn't look like it. Which country comes to your mind spontaneously?

Client:
(Hesitates) None. Somehow ... *(Seems to be grappling with a thought that he can hardly believe)*

Therapist:
Just say what comes to your mind spontaneously.

Client:
I can hardly believe it, but the word "gypsy" keeps popping into my head all the time. And that would explain a lot.

Therapist:
Do you know anything about your great-grandfather?

Client:
All I know is that my grandfather did not know his father. He was always a secret. My great-grandmother never talked about him according to my father.

Therapist:
Then slip into the role of your great-grandfather and say to his son: "My son, I fathered you and then moved on."

Client:
My son, I fathered you and then moved on.

Therapist:
How does that feel?

Client:
Really good. Totally true. And my grandfather can really see his father now.

Therapist:
Stay in the role of your great-grandfather, and he says to his son: "My son, our home is the road, our roots have wheels, we are at home everywhere and nowhere."

Client:
My son, our home is the road, our roots have wheels, we are at home everywhere and nowhere.

Therapist:
How does that feel?

Client:
Really good. Now I know why I prefer to stay in hotels and love driving.

Therapist:
How does your grandfather feel?

Client:
Good. He just doesn't understand why he was never allowed to talk about his father.

Therapist:
Then imagine, your grandfather's mother standing in front of him and she says to him: "My son, I had a fling with a gypsy."

Client:
My son, I had a fling with a gypsy.

Therapist:
And you are the result of it.

Client:
And you are the result of it.

Therapist:
I was ashamed of this.

Client:
I was ashamed of this.

Therapist:
But now I realize that it was fortunate for you that we had something together.

Client:
But now I realize that it was fortunate for you that we had something together.

Therapist:
You may have him as your father now.

Client:
You may have him as your father now.

Therapist:
And I also respect him in you.

Client:
And I also respect him in you.

Therapist:
He will always be your father.

Client:
He will always be your father.

Therapist:
How does that feel?

Client:
Really good.

The idea of roots that have wheels came to me spontaneously when I was confronted with this problem for the first time in a seminar. Since then, I have seen three other cases where the ancestors were travelers. Interestingly, even homelessness offers a kind of home, presumably due to belonging to an ethnic group.

There was one case which spanned several generations in which a Gypsy fathered a child with a permanent resident. The phrase "My son, I have begotten you and then I moved on" was cheerfully accepted by the sons across the board and made them strong.

Incidentally, if you suspect having roots in another country or a different ethnic group could simply be wishful thinking, I have two counterarguments for you:

- If someone from Switzerland or Holland spontaneously gets an internal image of a German ancestor, and that occurs often, then wishful thinking is rather unlikely, since Germany is not the home country of choice for those people.

- Even if it were wishful thinking, please remember: There is no objective reality anyway. And it is our duty as therapists to work with the subjective reality of the client and to do everything we can to help make him strong.

Since I found out that my great-great-grandfather was a German servant on a Swiss farm who had a fling with the farmer's wife, I not only have an explanation for my great-grandfather's suicide, but many of my own problems that were resistant to therapy vanished into thin air in one sweep. And in my mental picture all of my male ancestors are now big and strong, and they weren't before.

I know I run the risk of my parents and siblings reading this and telling me I'm crazy. But I just wanted to show you that I'm also speaking from personal experience here.

(Note: My younger brother has now read the book, and the idea of having German roots resonated deeply within him!)

Example 6: A Child from a Rape

Therapist:
Slip into the role of your great-grandmother and she says to her mother, "Hi, Mom".

Client:
Hi, Mom.

Therapist:
How does that make your great-grandmother feel?

Client:
Bad.

Therapist:
What does that mean?

Client:
There's an icy cold feeling coming from her.

Therapist:
Stay in the role of your great-grandmother and say, "Mom, I would have liked to have had more love and security from you."

Client:
(Is barely able to utter the sentence)
Mom, I would have liked to have had more love and security from you *(intense abreaction)*

Therapist:
How does your great-great-grandmother feel when she hears that?

Client:
(In tears) She's so ice cold; it's horrible.

Therapist:
Then imagine your great-great-grandfather is there and your great-great-grandmother says to him, "Look, this is the child

that we conceived."

Client:
She can't say that. She can't even look him in the eye.

Therapist:
She should say it first and then evaluate it.

Client:
They didn't conceive the child together.

It is very important that the therapist remains clear. A poorly trained therapist would now assume that the great-great-grandfather is not the biological father. But that was clearly defined from the beginning: When I talk about the father, I mean the biological father. Therefore, there must be another problem:

Therapist:
Stay in the role of your great-great-grandmother and she says to your great-great-grandfather, "You raped me."

Client:
(A massive abreaction shows that the therapist has hit the nail right on the head. Long pent-up anger and grief can finally be released.)

Therapist:
(Once the client can respond again) And then she says to him, "I didn't even know you."

Client:
I didn't even know you.

Therapist:
Is that true?

It is important to find out whether it was a "domestic" rape, i.e. the great-great-grandmother was raped by her husband, or if the rapist was a stranger. The latter is even harder for the client to accept as you can imagine. And thus it needs a different set of resolving sentences.

Client:
Yes, that's true.

Therapist:
Then she says to him, "You hurt me so much that I could never be happy again."

Client:
You hurt me so much that I could never be happy again.

Therapist:
Is that true?

Client:
Yes, that's true.

Therapist:
But something good came out of it. Look, this is our daughter.

Client:
But something good came out of it. Look, this is our daughter.

Therapist:
How does the daughter feel?

Client:
Not good at all. She can't feel that it is something good.

Therapist:
Then slip into the role of your great-grandmother and say to her mother, "Mom, you were raped. That was a high price to pay so I could live."

Client:
Mom, you were raped. That was a high price to pay so I could live.

Therapist:
It's hard for me to see life as a gift.

Client:
It's hard for me to see life as a gift.

Therapist:
True?

Client:
Yes.

Therapist:
But look, I've given life to another generation. This is my daughter. And she gave life to her daughter. And she also has a daughter. The line has continued and all is well.

Client:
But look, I've given life to another generation. This is my daughter. And she gave life to her daughter. And she also has a daughter. The line has continued and all is well.

Therapist:
How does that feel?

Client:
Good. The great-grandmother is almost a little appeased.

Therapist:
Then slip into her role again and she says to her rapist: "You wanted something evil and something good came out of it. Good always prevails."

Client:
You wanted something evil and something good came out of it. Good always prevails.

Therapist:
How's that?

Client:
Very good. My great-great-grandmother is bigger.

Therapist:
And how does the great-great-grandfather, the rapist, feel?

Client:
He's bigger too.

At this point, it is important that resources are awakened for forgiveness. People who are not systemically trained may not understand this because they claim you can't forgive something like this.

However, people with systemic training know: Every person always does the best he can with the resources he has available at the moment. And they also know: Forgiveness is the alpha and omega of healing. If you withhold forgiveness, you are the one who carries the burden. This means he doesn't just make himself a victim once, but rather continues to play the role of the victim voluntarily. A victim is powerless and a doer is powerful. So forgiveness is the only way a victim can get his power back.

Therapist:
Step into the role of the great-great-grandfather and he says to your great-great-grandmother, "I just wanted to be seen."

Client:
I just wanted to be seen *(nods vigorously and starts to cry)*

Therapist:
In my family the men weren't respected.

Client:
In my family the men weren't respected.

Therapist:
True?

Client:
Yes.

Therapist:
I have put everything into turmoil with my violence, but I still wasn't seen.

Client:
I have put everything into turmoil with my violence, but I

still wasn't seen.

Therapist:
True?

Client:
Yes.

Therapist:
How does your great-great-grandmother feel now?

Client:
Now she's taking my great-great-grandfather by the hand and they're looking at their daughter and us descendants.

Therapist:
Good, and how do you feel?

Client:
I hate to say it but the man fascinates me.

Therapist:
You mean the rapist?

Client:
Yes.

Therapist:
Then say to him, "Great-great grandfather, your strength has made an impression on me."

Client:
Great-great grandfather, your strength has made an impression on me.

Therapist:
True?

Client:
Yes.

Therapist:
And I will use the power that I've inherited from you to do good things.

Client:
And I will use the power that I've inherited from you to do good things. *(Physiognomy of the client shows that this sentence is a breakthrough for her)*

Therapist:
How does that feel?

Client:
Incredible. I really feel completely connected to my ancestors.

This is just one of many examples. And I'd warn you against using it as a kind of template for every similar case. Each fate is different and the memorization of resolving sentences is pointless. For example, if the son of the client is suffering from schizophrenia, then the sentence, "The line has continued and all is well" may seem like a mockery, even if you, as a spiritually-oriented therapist, believe that everything has a deeper meaning. On the everyday level, all is not well for the client.

I wanted to share these examples with you to help you better understand the systemic principles that you learned during your training. Because if you do and when you've had enough practical experience, you will automatically find the appropriate resolution sentences.

Summary Check No. 2

- "Imagine your father is standing behind you; behind him is his father; and behind him his father, and so on. Thus, five generations of male ancestors. Each one has his hands on the shoulders of his child. Do you feel the energy that is flowing to you?"

- "Everything that I've been carrying for you, I'm giving back to you now. It's better off with you. I am but a child."

- "Look at your father, then at your grandfather, great-grandfather, great-great-grandfather, and great-great-great-grandfather. Does one of them come across as particularly masculine or very strong?"

- If so, "Say to the man, 'Dear XY, I could use a little more of your masculine energy.' Then slip into his role and say, 'I'm giving it to my child, he gives it to his, and so on, until it gets to you.' Then stand in front of your father again and feel how the energy is now flowing better."

- Important if the father is from another country: "Dad, I'm from (Italy), just like you. Germany has received me well. But my roots are in Italy and that feels good. My homeland will always have a place in my heart.

- For displaced persons: "(Silesia) can't do anything about it. (Silesia) is and always will be our home."

- For Gypsies: "My home is the road. Our roots have wheels. (You fathered me and moved on.)"

- Proceed with feminine powerhouse in the same fashion, except with regards to homeland. Instead of hands on shoulders, hands of the female ancestors are placed on their daughters' hips.

The masculine energy is needed to move forward, to stand one's ground, to make money, to assert oneself. The feminine energy is needed to deal with emotions, to make intuitive decisions and to think holistically.

Systemic Check No. 3: Organized Mental Picture of the Family of Origin

The third systemic check concerns the correct order in the family of origin. Mind you, this is about creating order in the "mental picture" of the family. This allows the client to find his place in life, regardless of how neurotically his family members behave on the day-to-day level and regardless of who is alive or dead.

It's best if I illustrate this using the family from Example 1:

Example 7

Therapist:
Let's set up your family of origin again around the center of the clock in a wide semicircle.

Client:
Where on the clock?

Therapist:
It doesn't really matter. They're standing close to each other in a slight semi-circle so that everyone can see each other. And your father is all the way to the right. To his left, left from his point of view, is his wife.
To her left is the oldest child, in other words, you. To your left is Teresa, the second oldest. And on the far left is Bernard, the youngest. Can you imagine that?

Client:
Yes.

Therapist:
Good. Then slip into the role of your father and he looks left to his family. Directly to his left is his wife, Elsbeth, and then the children according to age.

The client's mental picture (and that of the therapist) should now look something like this:

On the therapist's notepad:

Conjured in the minds of the therapist and client:

Therapist:
And the father says, "This is my place."

Client:
This is my place.

Therapist:
How does he feel about it?

I want to interrupt our example for a moment to give you a few important tips:

1. I want to reiterate again that this mental picture that we're building does not have to correspond to reality. The family can actually be

completely destroyed, individual family members may already be dead, contact may have been cut; none of this matters. If you have brought the mental picture of the family into order, you will understand why the NLP people say, "It's never too late for a happy childhood".

The neurolinguistic programmers may have come up with a technique, which is questionable in my opinion, that they call "Change personal history", but, the statement is one hundred percent true for systemic work. Remember: Systemic Check No. 3 is not about glossing over things or healing an entire family by remote treatment, but rather merely ensuring that the client comes to terms with his roots and reconnects to his ancestral "power source".

Your clients will probably say something like that. "It's as if I've finally been connected to the power" is a commonly heard phrase.

2. Due to the fact that both mother and father were involved in System Check 2 (male and female lines), some essential conditions have already been met for them to take their places in their chosen family. Often, however, there is still something slightly open between the two as a couple, as I will show you shortly when we continue with our example.

3. If a child doesn't agree with his place within the family, there can be several reasons for it:

- He mistakenly thinks that birth order has something to do with "value", so that, for example, second place is worse than first. I'll show you how to clarify that in the example.

- He is carrying something for the parents and is of the opinion that he is entitled to a "better" place because of it. More about that later on.

- He took the place of a parent. Reasons for this may include a parent who is too weak, is not with the family mentally, has died or moved away.
  This too needs to be clarified and put into order.

- The child's place is actually not the right one, for example, because a miscarriage was unconsciously perceived as a family member but is hushed on the everyday level or because a vanished twin plays a role.

I know this is a lot of information at once. It's high time that we return to our example:

Client:
It feels okay for my dad.

Therapist:
Stay in the role of your father and he says to his wife, "Elsbeth, I took you as my wife. I'm your husband. And these are our children, Markus, Teresa and Bernard."

Client:
Elsbeth, I took you as my wife. I'm your husband. And these are our children, Markus, Teresa and Bernard.

Therapist:
How does the father feel?

Client:
Good. He just wants his wife to finally look at him.

Therapist:
Slip into the role of Elsbeth and she says to her husband, "Martin, I took you as my husband. I'm your wife."

Client:
She doesn't want to say that.
(makes a stubborn face)

Therapist:
Then she should say, "I didn't want to marry you."

Client:
I didn't want to marry you.

Therapist:
True?

Client:
Yes.

Therapist:
I married you anyway.

Client:
I married you anyway.
(*smiles*)

Therapist:
How does that feel?

Client:
(*Laughs relieved*) Good! It's true.

Therapist:
And I gave you three children.

Client:
And I gave you three children.

Therapist:
Although you didn't forced me.

Client:
Although you didn't forced me.

Therapist:
How does it make Elsbeth feel?

Client:
Yeah, good. It's true. Nobody forced her.

Therapist:
Then she says, "Too bad it didn't work out better."

Client:
Too bad it didn't work out better.

Therapist:
I assume responsibility for my part and I leave your part with you.

Client:
I assume responsibility for my part and I leave your part with you.

Therapist:
How does it make Elsbeth feel?

Client:
Good. It's freeing.

Therapist:
How does it make Martin feel?

Client:
It's good for him too.

Therapist:
Then slip in the role of Martin and he says to his wife, "Too bad it didn't work out better between us. I assume responsibility for my part and I leave yours with you."

Client:
Too bad it didn't work out better between us. I assume responsibility for my part and I leave yours with you.

Therapist:
Then Elsbeth should say to her husband, "Maybe I can learn to love you."

Client:
Maybe I can learn to love you.

Therapist:
How does it make Elsbeth feel?

Client:
Good. I have the feeling she's seeing her husband for the first time.

Therapist:
Then she says, "Whatever happens between us, we will always be connected through our children."

Client:
Whatever happens between us, we will always be connected through our children

Therapist:
Martin, I've never really seen you.

Client:
Martin, I've never really seen you.

Therapist:
Is that true?

Client:
Yes.

Therapist:
Try the following sentence. You'll realize immediately if it's right: "I'm only just starting to see you now."

Client:
I'm only just starting to see you now.

Therapist:
Does the sentence feel right to you?

Client: *(Nods)*

I'd like to stress again that this intervention is possible if one or even both of them are already dead. The idea here is to put the client's mental picture of his parents in order.

Please make sure your clients understand why this is being done, so they do not return to everyday life with false expectations, only to be disappointed when their parents are still as neurotic as before "in real life". But don't be surprised if your clients report unexplained positive changes in their family environment. This proves the old principle that a system has no choice but to change when part of the system changes.

Therapist:
Then slip into the role of Martin again, and he says: "This is my place."

Client:
This is my place.

Therapist:
How does that feel?

Client:
Good. Right. He's proud of his family.

Therapist:
Then slip into the role of Markus. He turns to his younger siblings and says, "I'm the firstborn."

Client:
I'm the firstborn.

Therapist:
How does that feel for you?

Client:
Good.

Therapist:
Then say, "You come after me."

Client:
You come after me.

Therapist:
How's that?

Client:
Good.

It is important to check each sentence to make sure it feels right to the client. You don't impose a solution on the client, but rather you work together to find the solution.

Therapist:
Then say, "This is my place."

Client:
This is my place.

Therapist:
How does that feel?

Client:
It's good for me.

Therapist:
What does that mean? Not for your sister?

Client:
No, she looks skeptical.

Therapist:
Then tell her, "Teresa, I was born in 1975, you in 1978.
That makes you my younger sister."

This logical argument is usually enough for the younger sibling to take his place. But be careful: Don't be dissuaded from your therapeutic care with expressions like "Yeah, it's okay" or "I accept that". That doesn't have anything to do with the proper acceptance of his or her place.

Client:
Teresa, I was born in 1975, you in 1978. That makes you my younger sister.

Therapist:
How does your sister feel about that?

Client:
She accepts it.

Therapist:
But she doesn't like it, does she?

Client:
No, not really.

Therapist:
Then say to her, "Teresa, second place is not worse than first. It's just different. And it belongs to you alone."

Client:
Teresa, second place is not worse than first. It's just different. And it belongs to you alone.

Therapist:
How does Teresa feel about that?

Client:
Yeah, it's okay.

Here, too, "okay" is too weak and doesn't prove that something has really been accepted wholeheartedly.

Therapist:
Okay isn't good enough for me. Slip into the role of Teresa. She goes to her father and says "Dad, the place next to you was free."

Client:
Dad, the place next to you was free.

Therapist:
And I flirted with the idea of taking it.

Client:
And I flirted with the idea of taking it.

Therapist:
True?

Client:
Yes.

Therapist:
But it does not belong to me.

Client:
But it does not belong to me.

Therapist:
It's Mom's.

Client:
It's Mom's.

Therapist:

What's between you and Mom is none of my business. I am just the child. And I'm going to go play now.

Client:
What's between you and Mom is none of my business. I am just the child. And I'm going to go play now.

Therapist:
How does Teresa feel about that?

Client:
Relieved. But she's afraid to go and play.

Therapist:
Then she should say to her parents, "Mom, Dad, I'm giving you back everything I've been carrying for you now. I am just the child."

Client:
Mom, Dad, I'm giving you back everything I've been carrying for you now. I am just the child.

Therapist:
And please give back what you're carrying for your parents.

Client:
And please give back what you're carrying for your parents.

Therapist:
For everyone is responsible for his own fate.

Client:
For everyone is responsible for his own fate.

Therapist:
And only for his own.

Client:
And only for his own.

Therapist:
How does Teresa feel about that?

Client:
Good. A huge burden just fell from her shoulders.

Therapist:
How do your parents feel?

Client:
Very good. They're bigger.

Not only does the one who has returned a burden become stronger, but the one who has to bear his own burden does as well. You will observe this phenomenon again and again. The following is an effective resolution sentence in this context:

Therapist:
Teresa should say to her parents, "I respect you by leaving your fate with you."

Client:
I respect you by leaving your fate with you.

Therapist:
How do her parents feel?

Client:
They're even stronger now.

Therapist:
Good. Then Teresa should go back to her place to the left of Markus and to the right of Bernard. And she says to her older brother, "Markus, you're the firstborn."

Client:
Mark, you're the firstborn.

Therapist:
I come after you.

Client:
I come after you.

Therapist:
How does Teresa feel about that?

Client:
Very good. That fits.

Therapist:
Then she says, "I'm second, and this is my place."

Client:
I'm second and this is my place.

Therapist:
How does Teresa feel about that?

Client:
Excellent. She feels really strong. And I don't have to feel guilty anymore about having taken her place away.

Therapist:
And you didn't. That was always your place.

Client:
Exactly.

Therapist:
Slip into the role of Teresa. She turns to her younger brother and says, "Bernard, this is our oldest brother Mark. I am second and you're third."

Client:
Bernard, this is our oldest brother Mark. I am second and you're third.

Therapist:
How does Bernard feel about that?

Client:
He's unhappy for some reason.

At this point, you can proceed similarly as with Teresa. You can try it logically ("I was born in 1978, you in 1980") or with the argument that the third place is not worse than the second. Finally, you can have Bernard return any possible burdens to his parents.

In the present case, however, all of these steps have only been partially successful. And so I want to show you another possibility. You have to know the following:

Embryological research says that the percentage of two or more fertilized eggs at the beginning of pregnancy is about 30 percent. But not more than five percent result in twins or multiple births. That means that almost one in three has lost a sibling in the first two months of pregnancy. In German, there is a lot of literature now on this subject. In English, there is some, for example, *"Womb Twin Survivors"* by Althea Margaret Hayton.

You can easily find out if your client has lost a twin. It goes like this:

> Therapist:
> Imagine slipping into the role of Bernard and I say to him: "Bernard, I'm going to count to three, and on three we are at the very beginning of your time in the womb just after the moment you were conceived. One, two, three. Are you alone in the womb or is there someone else with you? "

Do not worry that there may be clients who are interested in a vanished twin and thus fall prey to their wishful thinking. As an experienced therapist, you will immediately notice if the emotions that inevitably come into play when someone discovers that he has lost a twin are being feigned.

> Client:
> *(Upset emotionally)* There's someone with me.
>
> Therapist:
> Would it have been a girl or a boy? What was your first thought?
>
> Client:
> A boy.

Therapist:
And what do we want to call him? Just give me a male first name that you like.

Client:
Stephen.

Therapist:
Good. Imagine I could talk to Stephen and asked him, "Stephen, were you not able to come, or did you not want to?" What would Stephen say to me?

Client:
I couldn't.

Therapist:
Was there not enough room for both of you?

Client:
Yes.

Therapist:
And then you voluntarily withdrew?

Client:
Not entirely voluntarily. I was the weaker one.

In this case, two fundamentally different dynamics can present themselves:

- The twin withdrew more or less voluntarily, because there wasn't enough room for both of them. In this case, the surviving twin feels guilty, which may result in, among other things, his not being able to fully accept his life and not allowing himself to be successful and happy.

- The twin did not want to come, for example, because the family situation seemed too difficult. Then the surviving twin often feels deeply disappointed and lonely.

In this case we are dealing with the first variant. I'll tell you later how to deal with the second case.

Therapist:
Good. Markus, slip into the role of Bernard and he says to his twin brother: "Stephen, because you withdrew, I could be born. I thank you for that."

Client:
(In tears) Stephen, because you withdrew, I could be born. I thank you for that.

Therapist:
How does Bernard feel about that?

Client:
Bad. He misses his brother. And he has a guilty conscience. Why should he be allowed to live and not his brother?

I fall back here again on cathartic role-play:

Therapist:
Then imagine I could talk to Stephen and say, "Stephen, how does your brother's not wanting to accept his life make you feel?" What would Stephen say if he could talk?

Client:
That's ridiculous. I didn't withdraw for him to make nothing of his life.

Maybe you're wondering whether I just made up all of this. I can assure you: Your clients will make such statements again and again. I am amazed how often a resolution sentence comes from the clients themselves. The holistic approach of C.G. Jung is proven to be true again and again: Everyone has access to everything that is. What's not in his everyday personality (persona), is located in his psychological shadow. And in a light trance, the whole shadow area becomes accessible.

Therapist:
Bernard, you heard him. What do you think?

As you recall, I'm working with a client named Markus. However, he is currently in the role of his younger brother Bernard. I'm sure you've already noticed the great advantage, aside from a few disadvantages, to working systemically in a trance compared to setting up human substitutes. Since the client has to play each role himself, he experiences not only the emotions, but also all of the remaining resources of each role. There's no better intervention for awakening mutual understanding.

Client:
Yeah, he's right.

Therapist:
Then stay in the role of Bernard and say to Stephen, "I'll make the best of it in your honor."

Client:
I'll make the best of it in your honor.

Therapist:
And imagine Bernard showing Stephen in the near future everything he's done in his life. He lets his twin brother share his life. How does that feel?

Client:
Great, finally he doesn't feel alone anymore.

Therapist:
Would Stephen have been his younger or older brother? Which one feels right?

Client:
His older.

Therapist:
Good. Then imagine Stephen is standing between Teresa and Bernard. Stay in the role of Bernard; he says to his brothers and sisters, "This is my twin brother Stephen. He is the third and I'm the fourth. Here is my place."

Client:
This is my twin brother Stephen. He is the third and I'm the fourth. Here is my place.

Therapist:
How does Bernard feel about that?

Client:
Super. It's as if he's grown roots.

Therapist:
How do the older siblings feel?

Client:
They feel great too. They're happy for Bernard.

Therapist:
Then slip into the role of Bernard again and say to his brothers and sisters, "I like being the youngest."

Client:
I like being the youngest.

Therapist:
How does that feel?

Client:
Really good.

Therapist:
Look carefully at the family members again. Is something unresolved somewhere?

Client:
No. They're all totally happy and strong.

Systemic Check 3 is about each client feeling that he belongs to his family. This means the "real" and thus biological family, of course. And this works just as well with orphaned children; even those who don't know who their parents are. In Systemic Check 1 that would sound something like this:

Example 8 (Orphan)

Therapist:
I know you don't know anything about your parents. But just imagine they were here. Your father is standing in front of you and your mother is to the right of him, on the right from your point of view.
And say to them, "Mom, Dad, unfortunately, I don't know anything about you."

Client:
Mom, Dad, unfortunately, I don't know anything about you.

Therapist:
I only know that you, Dad, fathered me and that you, Mom, gave birth to me.

Client:
I only know that you, Dad, fathered me and that you, Mom, gave birth to me.

Therapist:
How does that feel?

Client:
Good. Emotional.

Therapist:
What do you mean?

Client:
I feel like I have a relationship with my parents for the first time. I just want to know why they gave me up for adoption.

Therapist:
Imagine I could talk to your mother and say, "Why did you give your child up for adoption?" What would she say if she could talk?

Client:
She's very sad.

Therapist:
And what does she say?

Client:
I would have liked to have kept you.

Therapist:
And why didn't that work?

Client:
She was still really young. And my father ...

Therapist:
What about him?

Client:
I don't know.

Therapist:
Then let's ask him, "Why did you agree to give your child up for adoption?"

Client:
I wouldn't have been able to take care of her. I didn't earn much and had no education.

Therapist:
And later? You could have come to get your daughter later.

Client:
I would have liked to. But you're not allowed to. You're not allowed to hurt a child that much twice.

Therapist:
And your mother? Is this what she thinks too?

Client:
(*Starts to cry*) Yes, I would have loved to have had you with me. It was hard to leave her with her foster parents.

Therapist:
Say to your parents, "Otto and Karin took good care of me."

Otto and Karin were her foster parents. If they did not take good care of the child, however, you would have to find other phrases, such as "Growing up with Otto and Karin was very difficult for me." The principle is always: "First, express what is." That alone provides more relief than is commonly believed.

> Client:
> Otto and Karin took good care of me.
>
> Therapist:
> But you are my parents and always will be.
>
> Client:
> But you are my parents and always will be.
>
> Therapist:
> How does that feel?
>
> Client:
> Good. But I have a bit of a guilty conscience concerning my adoptive parents. As if I don't appreciate what they did for me.
>
> Therapist:
> What do you call Otto and Karin?
>
> Client:
> Mom and Dad.

There are different views on this: Many systemic experts think the adoptive or step-parents shouldn't be called "Mom" and "Dad", but rather by their first names, so that the space stays open for the biological parents in the mental picture. In my experience, it is very effective at least to use their first names in the resolution sentences creating a healthy distance and the relief of burden:

> Therapist:
> Say, just for the duration of this exercise, "Otto, Karin, thank you for caring for me. Thanks to you, I was able to survive."
>
> Client:
> Otto, Karin, thank you for caring for me. Thanks to you I was able to survive.

Therapist:
I bear your name as a sign of love and gratitude.

Client:
I bear your name as a sign of love and gratitude.

Therapist:
"But these two here are my parents," and point to your parents.

Client:
But these two here are my parents.

Therapist:
And they always will be.

Client:
And they always will be.

In the present case, Otto and Karin also had children of their own who were younger than the client. The client, however, was always treated as the firstborn. The result: The second oldest, who had been ousted from his place as firstborn in this family system, became very rebellious at school and at home early on and became addicted to drugs at age 16. A phenomenon that we repeatedly observe in patchwork families.

In Systemic Check 3, we're setting up a community or a patchwork family. And the orphan belongs on the far left or in last place, totally independent of her age. Incidentally, she will gladly take this place, if you have helped her to connect with her biological family properly before hand:

Therapist:
Stand to the far left of your host family and say: "This is my place in this community."

Client:
This is my place in this community.

Therapist:
Then stand in front of your foster family and say, "Thank you for letting me be your guest. Thanks to you I could survive."

Client:
Thank you for letting me be your guest. Thanks to you I could survive.

Therapist:
How does that feel?

Client:
Very good. And now the oldest finally has his place back.

By the way, the procedure is exactly the same for half-siblings. If there are both half-siblings as well as foster children, the half-siblings take precedence over the foster children, of course.

Those who have studied systemic therapy a long time know that a "place" never has a value. Each place has its rights and its duties. It's the same, if you'll allow me this brief detour into the subject of business management, for entrepreneurial teams. One of my clients once complained that his father, in whose company the client worked, had made him the boss but did not give him the full responsibility. I asked him who the head of the company was. They were both equal, was the answer. I asked if each of them owned exactly fifty percent of the company.

"No", said the client, his father held 51 percent and he held 49 percent. But it was agreed that they would reverse that at some point. "It doesn't matter," I said, "you're currently still number two. And obviously a bad number two, if you can't let your father be number one. If I were him, I certainly wouldn't make you number one until you've proven that you could be a good number two."

In companies, we have the freedom, thank God, to choose our place, and, if necessary, to fire people. It doesn't work that way for families, of course, because our place is determined at birth.

And by the way: You can draw your own conclusions about how practical it is to have family members work in the same company. In many cases, the problems are inevitable. Everything in life has a price. And if a child thinks that he can make his entry into professional life easier by sitting in a feathered nest, sooner or later he finds out that the price for this can be quite high.

Summary Check No. 3

- The father stands to the far right. If he doesn't feel strong enough there, put his parents behind him.

- If the father was too weak to ensure the family's security, his wife says to him: "You couldn't provide us with security. So I did it. But I feel more comfortable here to your left. Here is my place."

- If the parents' relationship was troubled:

    ▸ Too bad it didn't work out better between us.

    ▸ There were a lot of things that didn't have anything to do with you. It was my thing.

    ▸ I assume my part of the responsibility and I leave your part with you.

    ▸ For our children, it was fortunate that we were together.

    ▸ I confused you with my father/my mother. I'm sorry.

    ▸ I never really saw you properly.
    I'm only now starting to see you.

- All children give the foreign burden back to their parents in turn.

- With a Oedipus/Electra suspicion, "Mom/Dad, the place beside you was free. But it's not mine. I am just the child."

- The oldest child stands to the right of his siblings and to the left of his mother.
  "I am the firstborn. You come after me. "

- If the younger siblings do not accept their places, the firstborn says, for example, "Second place is not worse than first, it's just different. And it belongs to you alone. "

- Order sentences ensure that each sibling is happy with his place. If that is not the case, it often has to be clarified with the parents, "I am just the child."

- For communities:
  Half-siblings and foster children come at the very end, regardless of their ages! Half-siblings have priority over foster children. They say, "Thank you for letting me be your guest", to the foster family and connect to their biological parents.

Systemic Check No. 4: Detachment from the Family of Origin

The fourth Systemic Check is carried out very differently, depending on whether someone is still single or whether they have already established one or more chosen families.

The goal in each case is that the family of origin gives their "blessing" to the client's life. Might I remind you that we are speaking here of the "mental picture" of the family? So the client should not expect a neurotic family of origin to become the center of peace and security overnight. You'll see, however, that a neurotic family is much easier to bear when you have made peace with the mental picture of the family. Let's start with the "normal" case: Our client Markus from Example 1 is married for the first time and has fathered children:

Example 9

Therapist:
Take your wife Cornelia with your left hand, go a few steps away from your family of origin, turn around to your family of origin and say, "Please look kindly on me as I go my way with Cornelia."

Client:
Please look kindly on me as I go my way with Cornelia.

Therapist:
Are they all looking kindly?

Client:
Everyone except my mother.

Even if everyone is looking kindly at the client, I recommend that you always have them say the following phrases for good measure:

Therapist:
Go to your mother and tell her, "Mom, Cornelia is not taking anything away from you. She is just my wife. You are, and always will be, my mother."

You realize that we are talking about the level of order, right? On the everyday level, the new system will have precedence over the old one, of course. Here is a concrete example: When a man and his wife decide to go to the beach and his mother thinks it's a bad idea, it would be a violation of the systemic principles if the couple decided not to go on their beach vacation because of her.

Client:
Mom, Cornelia is not taking anything away from you. She is just my wife. You are, and always will be my mother.

Therapist:
How does your mother feel about that?

Client:
Now she's smiling. But she's not quite satisfied yet.

If this step does not cause the mother to look kindly, then not everything was cleared up thoroughly beforehand. That is, the mother must still feel an illegitimate claim to her son. In this case, you have to re-check whether something needs to be clarified between the mother and her husband, or whether the mother is still carrying her ancestors' burdens. I trust that you understand the approach to take in this case based on the previous chapter, and know what to do.
In the present case, however, even these measures did not present a complete solution. Therefore, let me show you another approach:

Therapist:
Slip into the role of your mother and she says to her son,
"Markus, I would've liked to have had a relationship like the one you have."

Client:
Markus, I would've liked to have had a relationship like the one you have.

Of course, You can only use this phrase when the mother was unhappy in her relationship, while the son hit the jackpot.

Therapist:
How does that make your mother feel?

Client:
Wistful. But relieved. Good, that she could say it.

Therapist:
Then she should say, "It's good that someone in the family made it work."

Client:
It's good that someone in the family made it work.

Therapist:
I'm glad that things are continuing well.

Client:
I'm glad that things are continuing well.

Therapist:
Maybe I'll learn how to do that too.

Client:
Maybe I'll learn how to do that too.

Of course, you can only use this sentence if the mother is still alive. Proceed in a similar fashion when one of the siblings doesn't look kindly. In this case, the most common cause is that the siblings are envious of their sibling's happiness.

And another thing: Although it is more common that the opposite-sex parent has a problem with the child's partnership, in other words, the mother with her son and the father with his daughter, it is always useful to say the sentence, "My wife/my husband isn't taking anything away from you", to both parents.

> Therapist:
> Imagine your two children are standing to the left of your wife according to their ages, and say to your family of origin, "Look, these are my two children, Kevin and Barbara, whom I fathered with Cornelia. The line has continued and all is well."
>
> Client:
> Look, these are my two children, Kevin and Barbara, whom I fathered with Cornelia. The line has continued and all is well.

I think it is unnecessary to emphasize that this phrase can only be used when everything has actually continued well. For example, if one of the children has a fatal disease, the statement wouldn't be well received. But by now, some good alternative phrases probably come to mind for such a case, right?

> Therapist:
> How does that make you feel?
>
> Client:
> Good. I'm proud.
>
> Therapist:
> And how's your family of origin?
>
> Client:
> They're happy.

Below I illustrate an important exercise for couples therapy. They can be very easily incorporated into Systemic Check 4:

Therapist:
Imagine that your mother is standing behind you and your wife is in front of you. Look at your wife, then at your mother; then at your wife again, and at your mom again. And then tell your wife: "Cornelia, you're my wife. And only my wife. "

Client:
Cornelia, you're my wife. And only my wife.

Therapist:
That's my mother. She is only my mother.

Client:
That's my mother. She is only my mother.

Therapist:
And I can distinguish between you both well now.

Client:
And I can distinguish between you both well now.

Therapist:
Is that true? Can you distinguish between them well?

Client:
Yes. And it was important to say that.

Therapist:
In what way?

Client:
I think I have often seen my mother in my wife. She likes that I now see her as a wife.

Do you understand the principle of the fourth Systemic Check? Now I'll give you a few variations:

Example 10: A client with no partner and no children who fears commitment

Therapist:
Take a few steps away from your family of origin and say, "Please look kindly on me as I go my own way."

Client:
Please look kindly on me as I go my own way.

Therapist:
Are they looking kindly at you?

Client:
Yes, but my mother thinks it's unfortunate that I don't have any children.

Therapist:
Would you like to have some?

Client:
Probably not. Although I like children, the price is too high to me.

Therapist:
You mean the loss of freedom?

Client:
Yes.

Therapist:
Good, then tell your mother, "Mom, I have decided not to have any children."

Client:
Mom, I have decided not to have any children.

Therapist:
I know that that has a price.

Client:
I know that that has a price.

Therapist:
And I'm willing to pay that price.

Client:
And I'm willing to pay that price.

Therapist:
Please look kindly on me and my decision.

Client:
Please look kindly on me and my decision.

Therapist:
Is she looking kindly at you?

Client:
Still not quite.

It helps of course if you have done a thorough history and know a lot about this mother. But you can fill in anamnestic gaps at any time by simply asking:

Therapist:
Imagine I asked your mother, "Sophia, would you say that you've lived your life as you would have liked? Or have you danced more to other people's tune?"
What would your mother say?

Client:
She would say, "I couldn't live my life. I've always done what other people wanted me to do."

Therapist:
Good, then slip into the role of your mother, and she says to her son, "Ralph, I was afraid to live my life."

Client:
Ralph, I was afraid to live my life.

Therapist:
I see that you are not afraid.

Client:
I see that you are not afraid.

Therapist:
And that makes me proud.

Client:
And that makes me proud.

Therapist:
You have my blessing.

Client:
You have my blessing.

Therapist:
How does your mother feel?

Client:
Very good. It's okay for her now. Now she can respect my decision.

This takes a lot of sensitivity on the part of the therapist. If you feel, for example, that the issue of children is not completely resolved for the client (please also take into account women's biological age, because to give a 45-year-old woman hope of having children of her own would be irresponsible), you can use the following phrases to "leave everything open":

Therapist:
Mom, I thought that you couldn't live your life because of us kids.

Client:
Mom, I thought that you couldn't live your life because of us kids.

Therapist:
True?

Client:
Yes.

Therapist:
Now I see that it didn't have anything to do with us kids.

Client:
Now I see that it didn't have anything to do with us kids.

Therapist:
Maybe I'll reconsider having children.

Client:
Maybe I'll reconsider having children.

Therapist:
How does that feel?

Client:
It feels good. I feel so ... free.

Since the client also had a fear of commitment, I explored whether this problem had something to do with his mother:

Therapist:
Please try out the sentence, "Mom, I've refrained from having a serious romantic relationship until now to please you."

Client:
Mom, I've refrained from having a serious romantic relationship until now to please you.

Therapist:
Does that feel right?

Client:
(Surprised) Yeah, sort of.

Therapist:
But now I can distinguish between you and a partner and know that she doesn't take anything away from you.

Client:
But now I can distinguish between you and a partner and know that she doesn't take anything away from you.

Therapist:
What does this sentence do with you?

Client:
Now a relationship is starting to sound interesting to me. Somehow I just ...

Therapist:
Somehow what?

Client:
Somehow I'm just afraid that a woman could dominate my life.

Therapist:
Then say to your mother: "Mom, as a child I was dependent on you."

Client:
Mom, as a child I was dependent on you.

Therapist:
That's true, right?

Client:
Yes, of course.

Therapist:
And I've been afraid of being just as dependent in a romantic relationship.

Client:
And I've been afraid of being just as dependent in a romantic relationship.

Therapist:
True?

Client:
Yes.

Therapist:
But now I see: A partner is an equal. And each is equally dependent on the other.

Client:
But now I see: A partner is an equal. And each is equally dependent on the other.

Therapist:
How does that feel?

Client:
Very good. These are really new perspectives.

Therapist:
Then slip into the role of your mother, and say to her son, "Ralph, the place at your side is now vacant."

Client:
Ralph, the place at your side is now vacant.

Therapist:
How does that feel?

Client:
Good. Really good. I feel really happy now.

To conclude this chapter, I would like to demonstrate a more complex constellation. The client was married for the third time. With his first wife (Gabriela) he had two children (Charles and Ursula), who were grown by this time. His second wife (Marlene) was childless and died of cancer. He had a six-year-old son (Maury) with his third wife (Jean), who also brought two children into the marriage (Peter, 14 and Marianne, 12).

Please remember that Systemic Check 4 is not concerned with the clarification between the individual wives; that isn't done until Check 6. First, you need to call on the understanding of the family of origin for the different chosen families:

Example 11: A "Patchwork Happy" Client

Therapist:
Put Jean on your left. Maury stands to the left of her.

And tell your family of origin, "Look, this is Jean, my third wife. I have fathered Maury with her."

Client:
Look, this is Jean, my third wife. I have fathered Maury with her.

Therapist:
This is Marlene. I was with her before.

Client:
This is Marlene. I was with her before.

Therapist:
Unfortunately, she died too soon.

Client:
Unfortunately, she died too soon.

At this point, the client was crying because we hadn't cleaned up this part of his past yet. I'll show you how to handle it later.

Therapist:
And this is my first wife Gabriela. I fathered Charles and Ursula with her.

Client:
And this is my first wife Gabriela. I fathered Charles and Ursula with her.

If a client's parent was similarly active in producing patchwork families, you can do a lot of good with this sentence:

Therapist:
Dad, I've done it just like you.

Client:
Dad, I've done it just like you.

Therapist:
I founded several families too.

Client:
I founded several families too.

Therapist:
How does that feel?

Client:
Good. My father is winking at me. It makes me feel really well connected to him. I have always blamed myself before.

Therapist:
What did you blame yourself for?

Client:
For being so promiscuous.

Therapist:
And now?

Client:
Now it's okay. Something good came out of it. Except with Marlene; that went wrong.

You could just ignore this remark if you wanted to. But, of course, a thorough therapist uses every opportunity to put things "in order":

Therapist:
Imagine I could ask Marlene, "Marlene did your death have anything to do with your husband?" What would she say?

Client:
(Suddenly realizes something) I think she went with her mother. She died when Marlene was twelve years old.

Therapist:
Then slip into the role of Marlene and say: "Ralph, my death had nothing to do with you."

Summary Check No. 4

- The male life partner is put on the right, the female life partner on the left, then say to the family of origin, "Please look kindly on me as I go my way with XY."

- If the mother isn't looking kindly at the son, "Mom, XY isn't taking anything away from you. You are and will always be my mom. XY is only my wife."

- Look at mother, look at partner, look at mother, look at partner. Then say, "You're my mother and only my mother. That is my wife and only my wife. And I can differentiate between you two well now."

- Proceed in the same way if the father isn't looking kindly on the daughter. This exercise is also a very effective exercise in couples therapy.

- If a sibling isn't looking kindly, find out why. Then "say what is" and follow up with resolving sentences.
  Example: "My brother, I would also have liked a relationship like the one you have. It's nice that at least someone in the family managed it. Maybe I'll even learn how to do it too. "

Systemic Check No. 5: Actual State of the Chosen Family

The fifth Systemic Check concerns the same thing as the first, only this time we look at the actual condition of the chosen family, i.e. the spouse and, if present, the children.

If you don't have much time for therapy, this is the check you can omit because the principle has already become clear in Check 1. Nevertheless, it can help your clients to see how his family of choice evolved. The following example proves that Systemic Check 5 can provide your client important insights that they otherwise wouldn't have access to:

Example 12

Therapist:
You remember the clock face that is about thirty feet in diameter. Imagine we put you and your wife Lena on there at the time when you already were together but didn't have any children yet. Where would you put Lena, near what number?

Client:
On the one.

Therapist:
Directly on the one or a little towards the center?

Client:
Directly on the one.

Therapist:
And where do we put you?

Client:
To Lena's right.

Therapist:
So, in the direction of the twelve?

Client:
Yes.

Therapist:
So close that you can touch each other?

Client:
Yes.

The client putting his wife on his left could indeed correspond to his true mental picture, but it could also be a sign that the client paid really good attention during Check 3 and wants to set up a "perfect relationship". Thank God the optical constellation of systemic work is only one factor. With the right questions you will immediately find out more:

Therapist:
Slip into your role. Your wife, Lena, is on your left at the time when you were already together but didn't have any children yet. How do you feel?

Client:
Good. Proud. She's the right one.

Therapist:
Slip into the role of Lena. Her husband, Ron, is on her right. How does she feel?

Client:
(Hesitates) Hmmm.

Therapist:
What was the first thought as soon as I asked?

Client:
I don't know if I'm making this up, but my first thought was "uncertainty".

Therapist:
Uncertainty with respect to what?

Client:
(Still in a tone of slight disbelief) Whether I'm the right one.

Therapist:
And what does it do to you when you notice this uncertainty?

Client:
It's not pleasant. I don't understand; I love her.

Therapist:
Good, then Kristin is born. Where do we put her?

Client:
In front of us.

Therapist:
What direction is she looking in?

Client:
At us. At Lena and me.

Therapist:
And how far away is she from you?

Client:
Almost six feet.

Therapist:
Is she standing exactly between you? Or is she closer to one of you?

Client:
No, between us.

Therapist:
Then slip into the role of Kristin. How is she?

Client:
She's fine.

Therapist:
How is Lena now that she has a daughter?

Client:
Now she has what she always wanted: A family. She's happy.

Therapist:
Has anything changed in her relationship with Ron?

You'll notice that I'm speaking about the client in the third person again. This helps him to better dissociate and slip into the role of his wife.

Client:
Yes, she feels more connected to him now.

Therapist:
Does that mean that the uncertainty in the beginning was due to the fact that she wasn't sure if you could have children with her?

Client:
It looks like it. I told her that I'd had the mumps at the onset of puberty and she knew that that can cause infertility. She really wanted to have children. That's probably what made her unsure.

Therapist:
How's Ron now that he has a daughter?

Client:
He's fine. He's proud. And he's also happy that his wife turns towards him more.

Therapist:
Then Leo is born. Where do we put him?

Client:
On the five.

Therapist:
Right on the edge of the clock, or a little towards the center?

Client:
About one-third towards the center.

Therapist:
And what direction is he looking in?

Client:
At Lena and me.

Therapist:
And how does Leo feel?

Client:
Set apart a little.

Therapist:
What do you mean?

Client:
Yeah, somehow like he doesn't belong.

Therapist:
Does this match the picture you have of Leo?

Client:
Yeah, sort of. He was a planned child. But we never got really close to him. It is as if he was mourning something and as if he'd built a protective shield around himself.

You can probably guess what the problem was, can't you? That's right, it was a vanished twin situation. You already know how to solve this. In Systemic Check 5, however, nothing is resolved; only the actual state is recorded.

Therapist:
How does Kristin feel about her younger brother?

Client:
A bit conflicted. On the one hand, she thinks it's exciting to have a living doll. On the other hand, he also takes away a lot of attention.

Therapist:
How does Ron feel about his son?

Client:
Good. Proud.

Therapist:
And how is Lena now that she has a son?

Client:
Also good. Now it's a real family in her opinion. But she would like him to be a little closer.

I want to impress upon you again: Resist the temptation to resolve tensions and entanglements in System Check 5. The idea is for the client to experience the situation into which each child was born. However, to do that you have to leave the situation unchanged!
Since System Check 5 is about recording the actual state of the family, there aren't very many variations. But a whole lesson is waiting for you in System Check 6...

Summary Check No. 5

- The same procedure as Check No. I, only this time with the chosen family (spouse, children)

- If the principles of the family of origin are already clear, this step can be skipped and you can go right to putting them in the correct order (Check No. 6).

Systemic Check No. 6: Order of the Chosen Family

The sixth Systemic Check not only brings order to the chosen family, but also clears up implicit and explicit tensions between any possible partners and ex-partners and their children. I'll start with the complex case from Example 11.

To refresh your memory: The client was married for the third time. With his first wife (Gabriela) he had two children (Charles and Ursula), who were grown by this time. His second wife (Marlene) was childless and died of cancer. He had a six-year-old son (Maury) with his third wife (Jean), who also brought two children into the marriage (Peter, 14 and Marianne, 12).

Example 13

Therapist:
Imagine that your present wife, Jean, is standing on your left and your son, Maury, is to the left of her. To Maury's left is his half-brother Peter and to Peter's left is Maury's half-sister Marianne. This is your current communal life. Say, "Here is my place."

Client:
Here is my place.

Therapist:
How does that feel?

Client:
Good. It just irritates me that Maury should have a better place than his older siblings.

Therapist:
They're not siblings; they're half-siblings. Do Peter and Marianne have the same father?

Client:
Yes.

Therapist:
And what's his name?

Client:
Jerome.

Therapist:
A Frenchman?

Client:
Yes.

Therapist:
Good, then let's leave your family for a minute and imagine Jean standing to the left of Jerome, Peter is standing to her left, and to the far left is Marianne. Can you imagine that?

Client:
So, from my point of view, Jean is standing to the left of Jerome?

Therapist:
No, from his point of view. Jean is on his left.

Client:
Yeah, I can imagine that.

Therapist:
Good, then slip into the role of Jerome and say to Jean, "Jean, we were a couple and we had two children together."

Client:
Jean, we were a couple and we had two children together.

Therapist:
Then we separated.

Client:
Then we separated. But that's not true; he cheated on her.

Therapist:
And as a result Jean and Jerome separated, right?

Client:
When you look at it that way, yes.

Therapist:
Jerome should say, "Too bad it didn't work out better between us."

Client:
Too bad it didn't work out better between us.

Therapist:
I assume my part of the responsibility and I leave you with your part.

Client:
I assume my part of the responsibility and I leave you with your part.

Therapist:
Through our children, we will stay connected forever.

Client:
Through our children, we will stay connected forever.

Therapist:
How does Jean feel about that?

Client:
Good. It was important to clear that up.

At this point you would have to repeat the same sentences in Jean's role before turning to the children:

Therapist:
Slip into the role of Jean and say to Peter and Marianne, "Peter, Marianne, what happened between your dad and me is none of your business. You're just the children."

Client:
Peter, Marianne, what happened between your dad and me is none of your business. You're just the children.

Therapist:
Jerome is and always will be your dad. And I am and always will be your mom.

Client:
Jerome is and always will be your dad. And I am and always will be your mom.

Therapist:
And I honor him in you.

Client:
And I honor him in you.

Therapist:
How do the kids feel about that?

Client:
It's nice for them. They feel relieved and it makes them stronger.

Therapist:
Good, then slip into the role of Peter and he says to his sister, "Marianne, I'm the first-born; you come after me."

Client:
Marianne, I'm the first-born; you come after me.

Therapist:
How does Peter feel about that?

Client:
Very good.

Therapist:
Then Peter should say: Here is my place.

Client:
Here is my place.

Therapist:
How does Peter feel?

Client:
Very good.

Therapist:
And how does Marianne feel?

Client:
Not so good.

Therapist:
Then stay in the role of Peter and say to Marianne, "Second place is not worse than first; it's just different. And it belongs to you alone."

Client:
Second place is not worse than first; it's just different. And it belongs to you alone.

Therapist:
How does Marianne feel now?

Client:
Better.

Therapist:
Good or better?

Client:
She accepts it. But with a bit of reluctance.

Therapist:
Then slip into the role of Marianne. She goes to her parents and says, "Mom, Dad, if I have been carrying something for you, I'm going to give it back to you now."

The phrase, "*If* I have been carrying something for you", is often better than, "Everything I've been carrying for you." It allows the client the freedom to think that he hasn't been carrying anything.

Client:
Mom, Dad, if I have been carrying something for you, I'm going to give it back to you now.

Therapist:
It's better off with you.

Client:
It's better off with you.

Therapist:
I am just the child.

Client:
I am just the child.

Therapist:
And I'm going to go play now.

Client:
And I'm going to go play now.

Therapist:
How does Marianne feel now?

Client:
A heavy burden falls from her shoulders.

Therapist:
How do her parents feel?

Client:
They think it's good. Their daughter should go play.

Therapist:
Good, then Marianne goes back to her place to the left of Peter. And she says to her brother, "You are the firstborn and I come after you."

Client:
You are the firstborn and I come after you.

Therapist:
How does Marianne feel now?

Client:
Now it's okay.

Therapist:
Then she should say, "I like being your younger sister; this is my place."

Client:
I like being your younger sister; this is my place.

Therapist:
How does Marianne feel now?

Client:
Good. Now she feels strong.

Therapist:
Then slip into the role of Jerome and say to his children, "Even though your mom is with Ralph now, she is still your mom and I am still your dad."

Client:
Even though your mom is with Ralph now, she is still your mom and I am still your dad.

Therapist:
And I honor your mother in you because half of you is made up of her, and the other half of me.

Client:
And I honor your mother in you because half of you is made up of her, and the other half of me.

Therapist:
How do the kids feel about that?

Client:
It's really good.

Therapist:
Good, then imagine the children are now standing in your communal home with you, Jean and Maury. To the left of Maury is Peter and to the left of Peter is Marianne. Slip into the role of Peter; he stands in front of you and says, "Ralph, thanks for letting me be your guest."

Client:
Ralph, thanks for letting me be your guest.

Therapist:
How's that?

Client:
Not so good for me.

Therapist:
Why not?

Client:
Because I try really hard to be like a father to him.

Therapist:
Then stay in the role of Peter and say to Ralph, "Ralph, you take good care of me. "

Client:
Ralph, you take good care of me.

Therapist:
And I'm grateful to you.

Client:
And I'm grateful to you.

Therapist:
But my father is Jerome.

Client:
But my father is Jerome.

Therapist:
And he always will be.

Client:
And he always will be.

Therapist:
How does Peter feel about that?

Client:
Good. It makes him strong.

Therapist:
And you?

Client:
I feel really good too. I just don't quite know...

Therapist:
Slip in your role and say to Peter, "Peter, I don't have to take care of you."

Client:
Peter, I don't have to take care of you.

Therapist:
What I do for you, I do out of love for your mother.

Client:
What I do for you, I do out of love for your mother. *(Sighs with relief)*

Therapist:
How do you feel now?

Client:
It's an unbelievable relief. I've always thought I had to be a better father than Jerome.

Therapist:
That's impossible. You can take better care of him. But you can't be a better father than the biological father.

Client:
Yes.

Therapist:
Then say to Peter, "I respect your father and your mother in you because you are made up of half of each of them."

Client:
I respect your father and your mother In you because you are made up of half of each of them.

Therapist:
How does Peter feel about that?

Client:
That makes him even stronger.

Therapist:
Whose name do they bear? Yours or Jerome's?

Client:
Mine. I adopted them.

Therapist:
And what's Jerome's last name?

Client:
Rossier.

Therapist:
Then slip into the role of Peter again and say to Ralph, "Ralph, I bear your name out of gratitude."

Client:
Ralph, I bear your name out of gratitude.

Therapist:
But in my heart I am and always will be a Rossier.

Client:
But in my heart I am and always will be a Rossier.

Therapist:
How does Peter feel about that?

Client:
Incredibly good.

Therapist:
Then he should say, "I am a Frenchman just like my father. And that feels good."

Client:
I am a Frenchman just like my father. And that feels good.

Therapist:
How does Peter feel about that?

Client:
He is bursting with pride. I think he's been missing that. He was always so disoriented and I couldn't explain why.

Incidentally, it would have been quite conceivable that Peter's disorientation would have later led to drug addiction. We often observe such issues in drug addicts. To be precise: Thus far, every drug case that I've met has had such familial entanglements.

You're probably wondering, "Shouldn't Peter be sent to therapy, as well?" At the risk of repeating myself, I say: Not by force. In general, it's enough when one part of the system changes. The rest changes by itself.

If Peter is open to therapy, it wouldn't hurt to work with him, of course. But I vigorously resist any form of "Helper Syndrome". In my experience, people who try to help even where help isn't asked for often do more damage than good.

Now the same procedure is carried out with the second child, Marianne. I admit it: It may sound a bit repetitive or even tedious. But if it seems boring to repeat processes that help clients find unprecedented feelings of happiness and to open doors for them that might otherwise have remained closed their whole lives, then I respectfully suggest you may be in the wrong profession.

Once you've connected both Peter and Marianne to their roots, it will not be hard for them to stand in front of their host family and say, "Thank you for letting us be your guests."

I can only remember one situation in which the foster child's surrogate thought the word "guest" meant "does not belong". I told him that we wouldn't have to have this discussion if he felt that he belonged to his biological family. It turned out that he had never fully accepted his father, who had left him and his mother early. Once this issue was resolved, in his role as the foster child, he no longer had a problem being referred to as a guest in his foster family.

> Therapist:
> Slip into the role of Maury, who is standing to the left of his mother. And Maury says, "Here is my place."
> Client:
> Here is my place.

Therapist:
How does Maury feel?

Client:
Great. Now he finally knows where he belongs.

Therapist:
Then Maury should say to his half-siblings, "Now that you've found your places, I can have mine too."

Client:
Now that you've found your places, I can have mine too.

Therapist:
How does Maury feel?

Client:
Very good. Even better than before.

Therapist:
And Peter and Marianne?

Client:
Also good. They are happy in their places.

The sequence for further treatment will vary with each therapist. You could now go on to Ralph's second wife and then proceed to the first or vice versa. The important thing is that you mitigate or resolve all areas of tension in the end.

Therapist:
Slip into the role of Jean. She goes to your first wife, Gabriela, and says, "Gabriela, I respect you as the first wife of my husband."

Client:
Gabriela, I respect you as the first wife of my husband.

Therapist:
You were there before me.

Client:
You were there before me.

Therapist:
Then she goes to your second wife, Marlene, and says, "Marlene, I respect you as the second wife of my husband.

You were there before me."

Client:
Marlene, I respect you as the second wife of my husband. You were there before me.

Therapist:
Because Gabriela left, you could come. And because you left, I was able to come.

Client:
Because Gabriela left, you could come. And because you left, I was able to come.

Therapist:
I thank you both.

Client:
I thank you both.

Therapist:
How do the two ex-wives feel?

Client:
Good. They feel respected. It was good that that was said.

Therapist:
Good. Then slip into your role and say to your first wife, "Gabriela, too bad it didn't work out better between us."

Client:
I can't say that.

Therapist:
Why not?

Client:
Because I don't think it's a shame. I'm happy with Jean now.

Therapist:
Does that mean you never wanted it to work out with Gabri-

ela from the beginning?

Client:
Of course, I wanted it to work out.

Therapist:
That's my point. And when things fell apart, it was a pity, right? You didn't know at the time about the good that would come out of it.

This Reframe is very important because you'll often hear the objection that things are indeed better with the current partner. It is not a matter of regretting something, but rather of showing respect for former partners and recognizing the efforts of both sides to make something good out of the partnership.

Client:
Too bad it didn't work out better between us.

Therapist:
I assume my part of the responsibility and I leave you with your part.

Client:
I assume my part of the responsibility and I leave you with your part.

Therapist:
Through our children, we will remain connected forever.

Client:
Through our children, we will remain connected forever.

Therapist:
After you, I was with Marlene. Unfortunately, she died. And now I'm together with Jean.

Client:
After you I was with Marlene. Unfortunately, she died. And

now I'm together with Jean.

Therapist:
I also have a child with her. Please look kindly upon me and my new family.

Client:
I also have a child with her. Please look kindly upon me and my new family.

Therapist:
Is she looking kindly?

Client:
Sort of.

Therapist:
Then slip into the role of Gabriela and she says to her ex-husband, "Ralph, too bad it didn't work out better between us."

Client:
Ralph, too bad it didn't work out better between us.

Therapist:
I assume my part of the responsibility and I leave you with your part.

Client:
I assume my part of the responsibility and I leave you with your part.

Therapist:
How does Gabriela feel?

Client:
She still doesn't understand why I left.

Therapist:
Then tell her, "Gabriela, my leaving had nothing to do with you."

Client:
Gabriela, my leaving had nothing to do with you.

Therapist:
Is that true?

Client:
Sort of, yeah.

Therapist:
Gabriela, I never really saw you properly.

Client:
Gabriela, I never really saw you properly.

Therapist:
Is that true?

Client:
Yes.

Therapist:
I was too busy with my own problems.

Client:
I was too busy with my own problems.

Therapist:
And try the sentence, "Only now am I starting to see you."

Client:
Only now am I starting to see you.

Therapist:
Does that feel right?

Client:
Yes.

Therapist:
And how does Gabriela feel now?

Client:
Great. She's blossoming. But she's also somewhat sad that we weren't able to resolve this earlier.

Therapist:
Then slip into her role and she says to her ex-husband, "It's a

pity, Ralph, a real shame."

Client:
It's a pity, Ralph, a real shame.

Please note: This is not about the client wanting to return to his ex-wife. It's simply making up for not having mourned that the relationship did not work out. Because as you know, divorces are often overshadowed by a lot of anger and rage, and the real feelings, which include grief, disappear with the stress of everyday life. It's incredibly liberating when the grief can be expressed with a simple. "It's a pity," and be made good.

Therapist:
Slip into your role and say to the children of your first wife, "Charles, Ursula, what happened between your mother and me has nothing to do with you."

Client:
Charles, Ursula, what happened between your mother and me has nothing to do with you.

Therapist:
You're just the children.

Client:
You're just the children.

Therapist:
Gabriela will always be your mother, and I will always be your father.

Client:
Gabriela will always be your mother, and I will always be your father.

Therapist:
How do Charles and Ursula feel?

Client:
It's really good. That was important to them.

Here too you should ensure that the children from his first marriage, Charles and Ursula, give their parents' burden back. You already know how to do that.

> Therapist:
> Slip into the role of Gabriela again and she says to your current wife, "Jean, I give Ralph now into your care. He is in good hands with you."
>
> Client:
> Jean, I give Ralph now into your care. He is in good hands with you.

A systemic facilitator once said that this was an inappropriate sentence because an ex-wife would never say that to a "successor". However, it's been my experience that this sentence has a strong conciliatory effect on all parties involved if you have cleaned up everything correctly beforehand. But again: You don't have to take my word for it; try it out and see for yourself!

> Therapist:
> Then slip back into your role and say to your second wife, "Marlene, you're my second wife."
>
> Client:
> Marlene, you're my second wife.
>
> Therapist:
> And you died young.
>
> Client:
> And you died young.
>
> Therapist:
> I blamed myself for a long time.
>
> Client:
> I blamed myself for a long time.

Therapist:
And asked myself what I did wrong.

Client:
And asked myself what I did wrong.

Therapist:
Today I know it had nothing to do with me.

Client:
Today I know it had nothing to do with me.

Therapist:
You just followed your mother.

Client:
You just followed your mother.

Therapist:
I honor your fate and respect your path.

Client:
(With tears in his eyes) I honor your fate and respect your path.

Therapist:
You will always have a place in my heart as my second wife.

Client:
(Crying harder) You'll always have a place in my heart as my second wife.

Therapist:
How do you feel now?

Client:
Very good. Liberated. Now I can let her go.

Therapist:
Then say to her: "Two years after your death I met my current wife, Jean."

Client:
Two years after your death I met my current wife, Jean.

Therapist:
I have a son with her. His name is Maury.

Client:
I have a son with her. His name is Maury.

Therapist:
Please look kindly upon me and my new family.

Client:
Please look kindly upon me and my new family.

Therapist:
And? Is she looking kindly?

Client:
Yes, very.

Therapist:
How does Jean feel when she thinks of your late wife?

Client:
She doesn't like to talk about her because she notices that it makes me sad.

Therapist:
Then slip into the role of Jean and say to Marlene, "Marlene, my husband still thinks about you often."

Client:
Marlene, my husband still thinks about you often.

Therapist:
Is that true?

Client:
Yes.

Therapist:
And sometimes it hurts me.

Client:
And sometimes it hurts me.

Therapist:
The living have no chance against the dead.

Client:
The living have no chance against the dead.

Therapist:
Is that true?

Client:
(Heaving a sigh) Yes, that's true.

Therapist:
Then slip into the role of Marlene and say, "My chance to participate in life is over. You still have that chance."

Client:
My chance to participate in life is over. You still have that chance.

Once again you can see how important it is that you as a practitioner have a mastery of the Reframes tool: The therapist provides a new meaning for the word "chance", which makes the client stronger.

Therapist:
And if you leave my place, you can have yours.

Client:
And if you leave my place, you can have yours.

Therapist:
How does that feel?

Client:
(Heaving a sigh) Sensational.

Therapist:
For both?

Client:
Yes, it's true... why didn't we think of that?

This is so good. So peaceful for everyone.

Therapist:
Then Jean should say to Marlene, "I respect Ralph and his grief for you."

Client:
I respect Ralph and his grief for you.

Therapist:
He will probably need quite a while before he can let you go.

Client:
He will probably need quite a while before he can let you go.

Therapist:
True?

Client:
Yes, absolutely. Now I can devote myself completely to my new family. Marlene is still there but she has her place. And I know that I can talk to Jean about her if I feel the need to.

Therapist:
Yes, it will probably work better now. And otherwise... you said that Jean is also open to therapy.

Client:
Yes, they actually sent me. And she said that if it helps me, she'd come too.

Summary Check No. 6

- The same principles of order apply as for the family of origin, and additionally:

- Current wife to ex-wife, "I respect you as the first wife of my husband. Because you left, I was able to come. I thank you for that."

- Ex-wife to current wife, "I now give XY into your care. He is in good hands with you."

- A similar procedure for ex-husbands.

- To children of the separation, "I respect your mother in you. She will always be your mother. What happened between her and me does not concern you. You're just the child. For you, it was fortunate that we were together. I will always be your father, and she will always be your mother."
  A similar procedure for fathers, "I respect your father in you", etc.

- The child says to the mother's new partner, "I don't have anything to do with you. This one is my dad. And he always will be."
  A similar procedure for the father's new partner.

- New partner says to the partner's child: "I don't have to care for you. What I do for you, I do out of love for my wife. You can keep it. This is your dad and he will always be."

- If a child's father is foreign: Handle the issue of the country of origin as previously discussed. This makes the child strong.

This concludes the Six Systemic Checks. If you should encounter situations in your daily work for which you can't find a solution, just send me an e-mail. I will take your questions into consideration in future editions and answer them if possible. You can find my current e-mail address on www.hpz-usa.com

The appendix contains a summary of the most important systemic rules. In addition, I would point you to the extensive existing literature and the equally extensive range of seminars on the subject.

I hope you enjoy your systemic work; if done correctly, it's a true blessing for the planet!

Appendix:
The Most Important Systemic Rules

I'd like to share a keynote presentation with you that I also use in my seminars. If you like it, I can send you the secret URL so you can have a look at the original. I also don't mind if you use the presentation in your own seminars, provided you always cite the source.

Just email me and let me know if you need the Keynote format (for Mac) or the PowerPoint format (Windows/Mac).

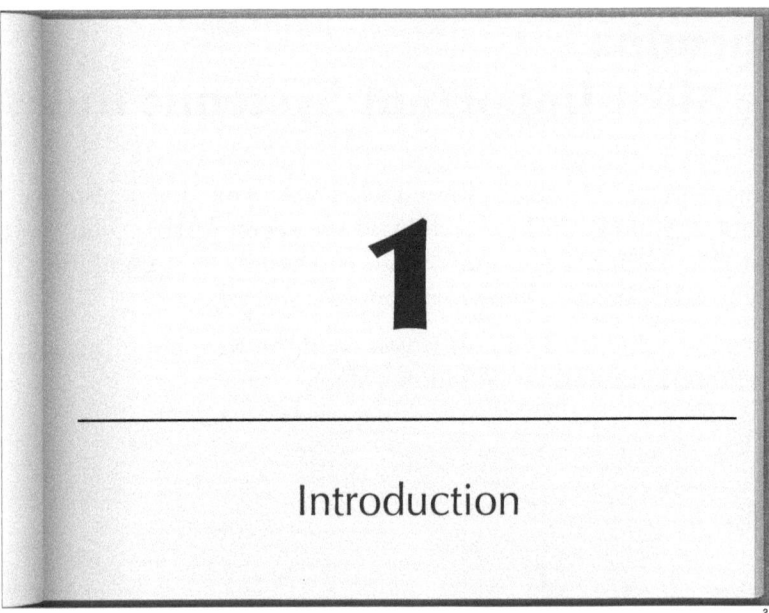

1

Introduction

2

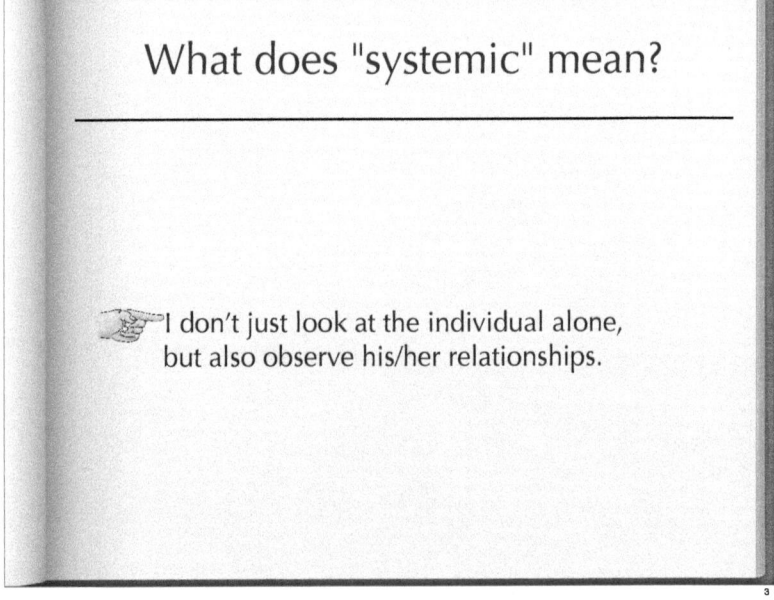

What does "systemic" mean?

I don't just look at the individual alone, but also observe his/her relationships.

3

How were the systemic rules developed?

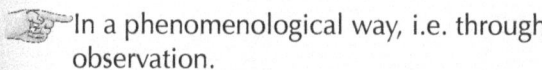 In a phenomenological way, i.e. through observation.

The main objective is to strengthen the client.

What makes the client strong is systemically "correct".

About this presentation

Most of the rules in this presentation were already well-known and can be found in books.

Some rules I (HPZ) discovered through observation and experience.
The reader is invited to test them out for himself.

2

Order

What is a system?

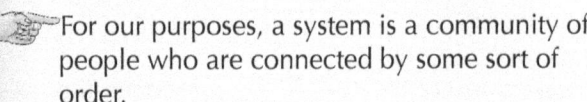 For our purposes, a system is a community of people who are connected by some sort of order.

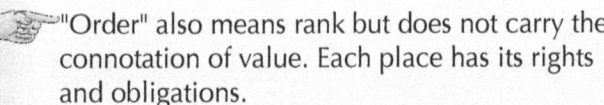 "Order" also means rank but does not carry the connotation of value. Each place has its rights and obligations.

If you want to represent the order graphically, the first place is on the far right and the last is on the far left (as seen by the family members).

Order – what for?

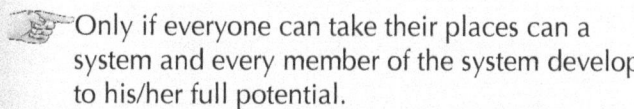Only if everyone can take their places can a system and every member of the system develop to his/her full potential.

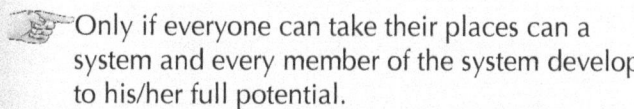Any violation of the order leads to suffering for EVERYONE involved.

Who makes the order?

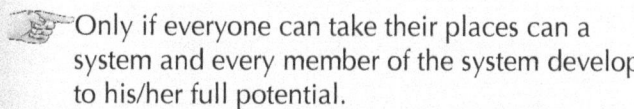In a company, the order is determined by the company structure. It can be changed at will.

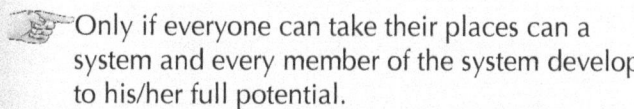In a family, the order seems to be determined by a law of Nature.

Order in the family

☞ On the far right is the one who is responsible for the security of the system externally. In our culture, this is usually the man.

☞ Then comes the one who is responsible for the "internal management". In our culture, this is usually the woman.

☞ Then come the (biological) children according to age. And then half-siblings and foster children.

10

3

Belonging

11

Belonging

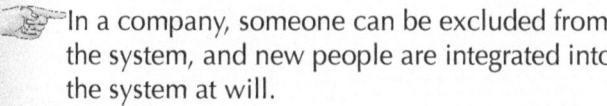In a company, someone can be excluded from the system, and new people are integrated into the system at will.

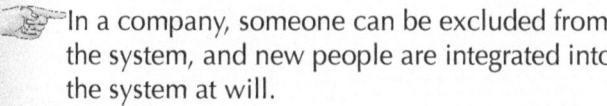In a family, you can't do that.
Each member belongs to the family regardless of their abilities and actions.

12

Disruption by exclusion

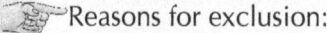If someone is excluded from a family system, the order is disturbed and one of the descendants will provide for the balance.
(often the cause of psychoses!)

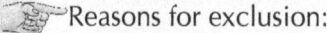Reasons for exclusion:

- Shame
  (Disability, illegitimate children, alcoholism, suicide, homosexuality)

- Guilt
  (Terrorism, wrongful inheritance, commitment of a felony, abuse)

- Pain
  (Early death of a child, tragic accident)

13

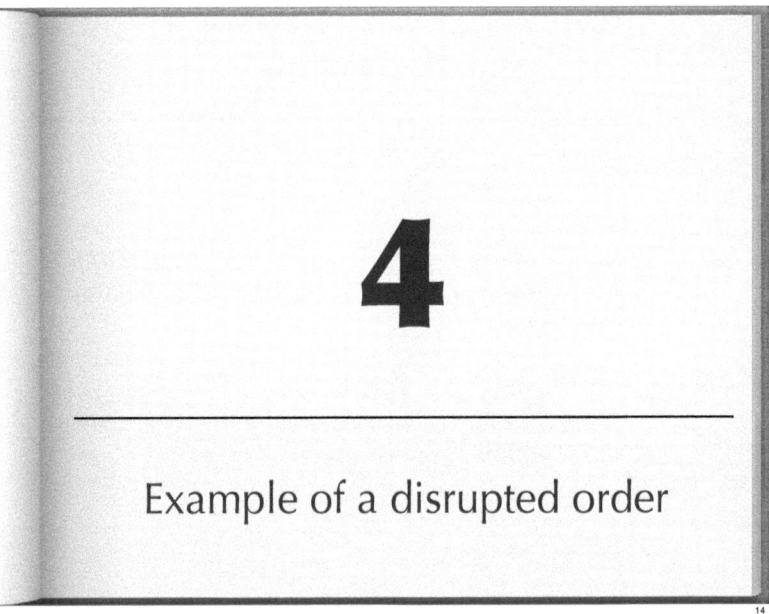

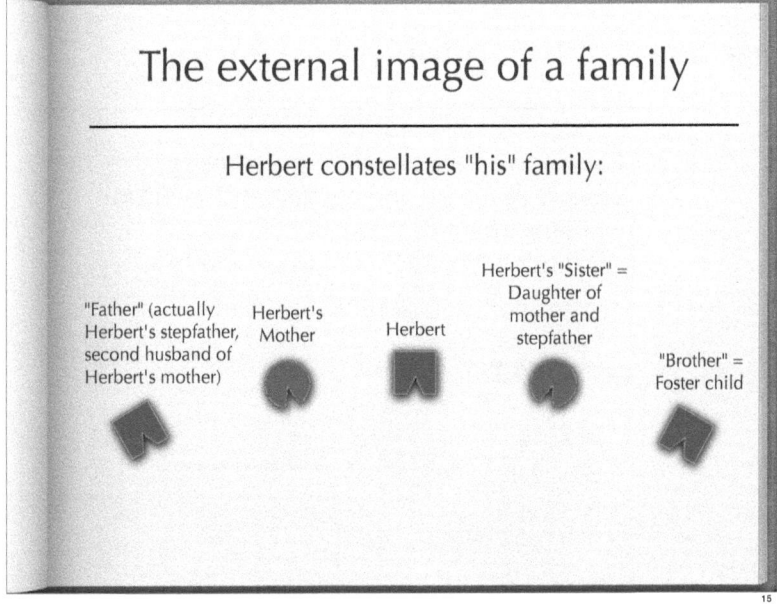

Caution!

☞ If Herbert's "internal picture" of the family is consistent with this external image, problems are inevitable.

☞ We can't usually change the external image of the family, but the internal picture we can. And anyone who has experienced this, knows how invigorating an internal image is when it is "in order".

16

Why the external image usually cannot be changed

☞ Members of the system are no longer alive.

☞ Members of the system are unknown.

☞ Members of the system are stubborn and unreasonable.

17

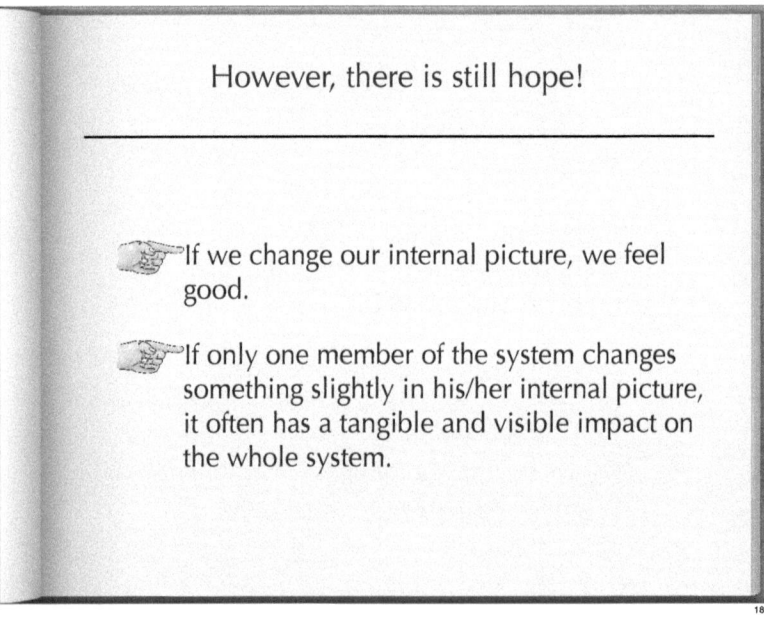

However, there is still hope!

☞ If we change our internal picture, we feel good.

☞ If only one member of the system changes something slightly in his/her internal picture, it often has a tangible and visible impact on the whole system.

18

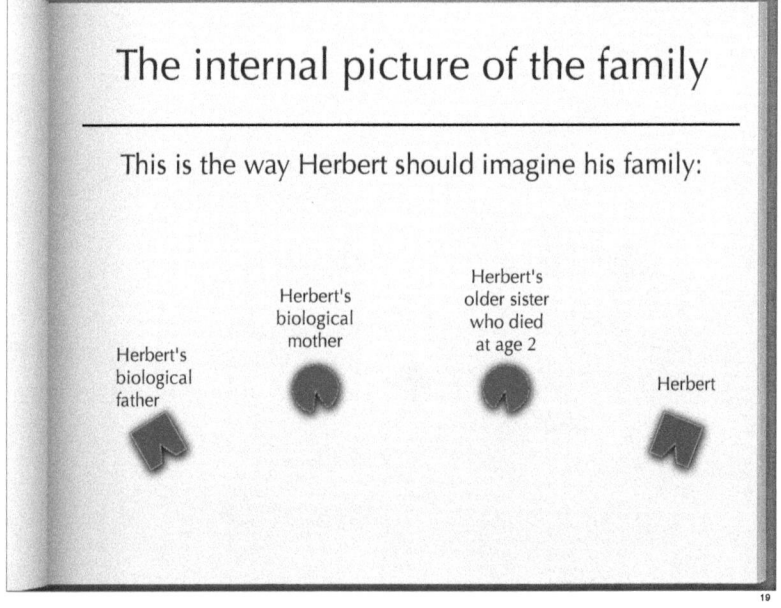

The internal picture of the family

This is the way Herbert should imagine his family:

Herbert's biological father

Herbert's biological mother

Herbert's older sister who died at age 2

Herbert

19

The order of a community

If Herbert wanted to bring order to his "foster family",
it would look like this:

Mother's
second
husband
(Peter)

Herbert's
biological
mother (Anna)

Only daughter
of Peter and Anna

Herbert,
has priority
independent
of age
over foster child

Foster
child

20

Finding one's place

Again: The point is that everyone finds his or her systemically right place.

A person's place does **not** have value.

The first place is no better than the second, it's just different ...

... and any fight against a person's true place leads to disruptions.

21

149

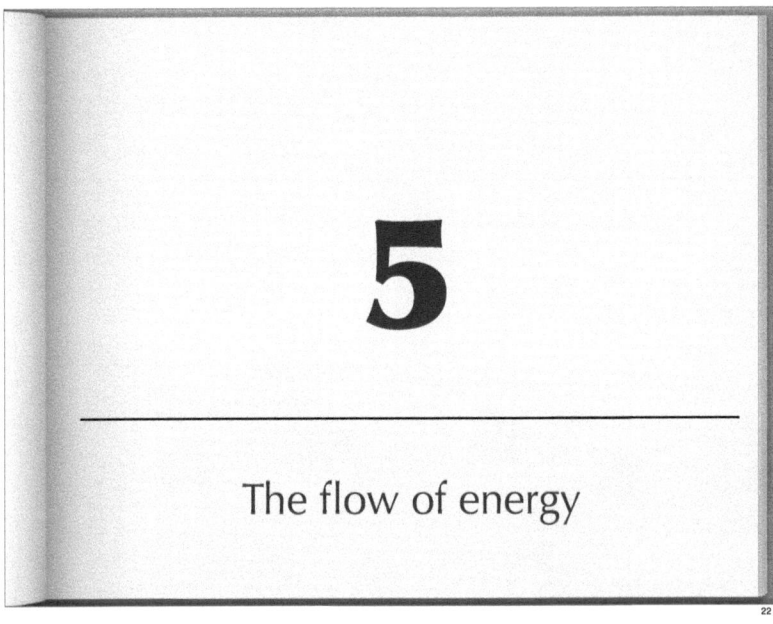

5

The flow of energy

22

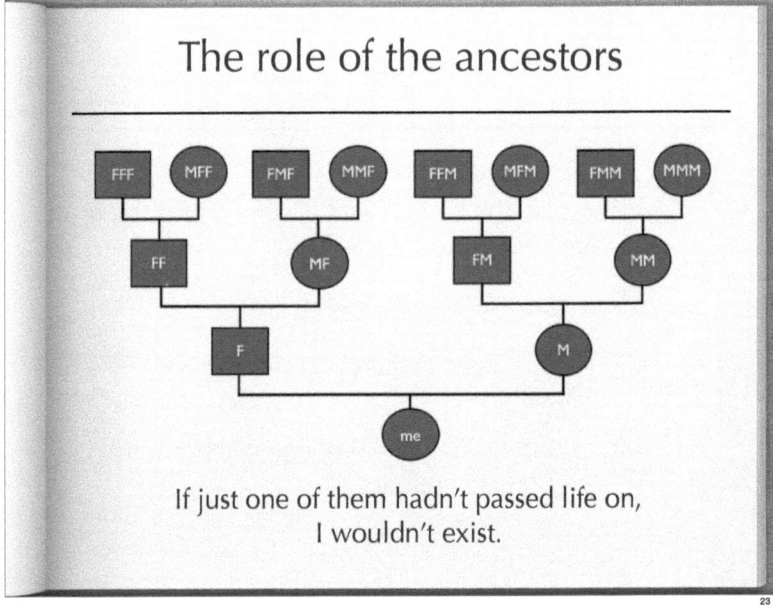

The role of the ancestors

If just one of them hadn't passed life on,
I wouldn't exist.

23

Connected instead of Bound

☞ Therefore, it is important that everyone feels connected to his ancestors.

☞ It's the only way he or she can feel his or her place in the family.

☞ And the only way he or she can find his or her place in the world.

24

The role of the parents (1)

☞ The father is always the man who fathered me.

☞ The mother is always the woman who gave birth to me.

☞ Biologically speaking, I am made up of 50% of my mother and 50% of my father.

☞ If I "demonize" or "deny" a parent, I am denying half of me.

25

The role of the parents (2)

☞ Whatever else my parents may or may not have done, they have given me life.

☞ I can accept this gift, or I can refuse it for some (systemically irrelevant) reason.

☞ If I refuse it, then I'm harming myself, my partner, and my children.

26

The energy flow

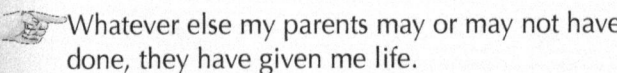

The energy flows from parents to children.
The parents give; the children take.

27

The following results from the principles of
"Order", "Belonging" and "Energy Flow":

☞ Everyone bears his own fate.

☞ Children often carry a burden for the parents.

☞ When the child accepts the order ("I am but a
child"), he feels relieved and can in turn relieve
his children of foreign burdens.

28

☞ Principle: Everyone is able to bear his own fate.
But only his own.

☞ Important sentence in this context:,
"I honor you by leaving your fate with you."

☞ If I don't allow a parent to be responsible for
his fate, I weaken him or her.

29

6

Entanglements

Basic dynamics of entanglements

1. "I'll follow you"

 "Since you're dead, I don't want to live either."

 "Since you're sick, I want to suffer too."

 "Since you're unhappy, I will forgo happiness."

 "Since you have lost your belongings, I will remain poor as well."

Basic dynamics of entanglements

2. "I'll do it for you."

 "Let me disappear instead of you." (e.g. Anorexia nervosa)

"I'd rather be sick so you can be well."

"I'd rather suffer from Dad's sexual violence than have you suffer, Mom." (Abuse)

"I'd rather die than let you die."
(e.g. The father is depressed and wants to die; the child gets a deadly disease)

"I would rather carry your burden."

32

Basic dynamics of entanglements

3. "I atone for you."

 Identification with a person who has been excluded from the family system.

Reasons for exclusion:

- Shame
  (Disability, illegitimate children, alcoholism, suicide, homosexuality)

- Guilt
  (Terrorism, wrongful inheritance, commitment of a felony, abuse)

- Pain
  (Early death of a child, tragic accident)

33

7

Small brainteaser

Relationship Level

Why are these statements proof of a fatal confusion
of the relationship level?

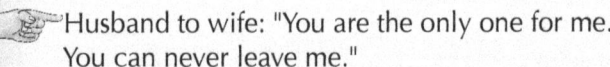Husband to wife: "You are the only one for me.
You can never leave me."

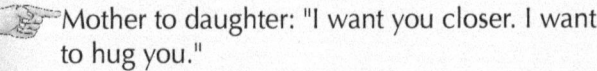Mother to daughter: "I want you closer. I want
to hug you."

Man to son: "You're my best buddy. I can talk
to you about everything."

8

The 6 Systemic Checks of HPZ

36

The 6 "Systemic Checks"

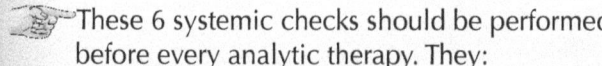

 These 6 systemic checks should be performed before every analytic therapy. They:

- Strengthen the client.

- Eliminate a great deal of therapy resistance.

- Provoke early abreactions (even for masters of denial), i.e., "The ice is broken quickly."

37

System Check 1
How was the family of origin formed?

How did the parents get along before they had children?

How was it when the first child was born?

Let the family form step by step and always check how everyone feels.

38

System Check 2a
Fixing the "masculine powerhouse"

▶ Line up five generations of male ancestors behind the client.

▶ Check to see whether the energy is flowing from father to child.

▶ If it's not flowing, work systemically until it flows.

▶ If these men remain small: Ask each of them where he is from and "repair the roots".

39

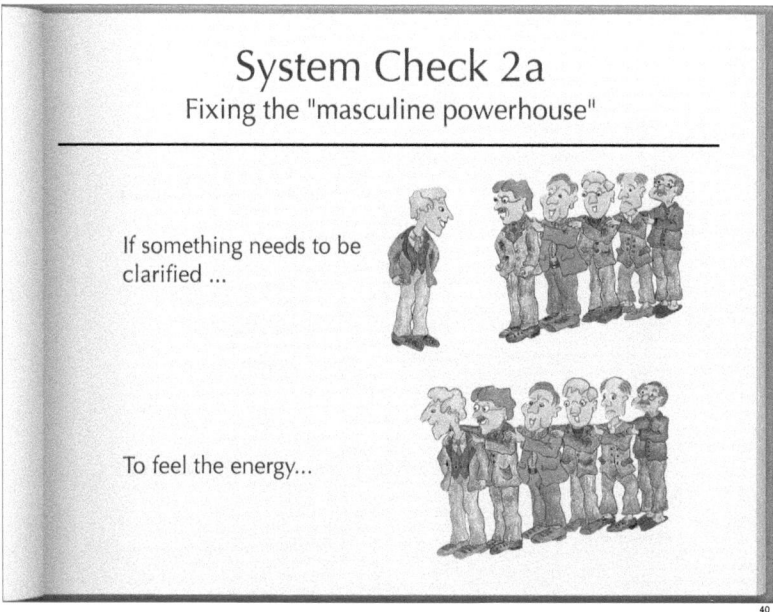

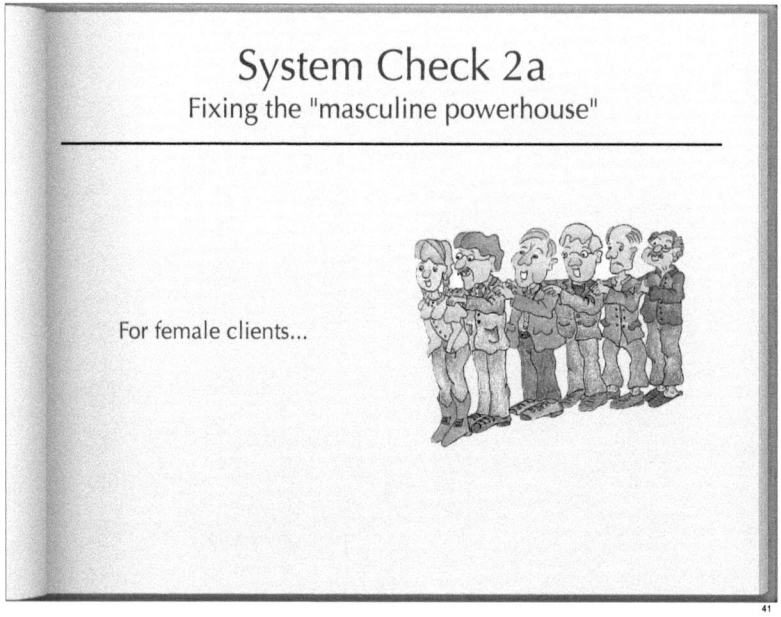

System Check 2b
Fixing the "feminine powerhouse"

- ▸ Line up five generations of female ancestors behind the client.

- ▸ Check to see whether the energy is flowing from mother to child.

- ▸ If it's not flowing, work systemically until it flows.

- ▸ If the women remain small, identify their roots.

42

System Check 2b
Fixing the "feminine powerhouse"

If something needs to be clarified ...

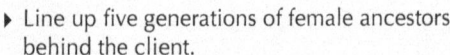

To feel the energy...

43

System Check 2b
Fixing the "feminine powerhouse"

For male clients...

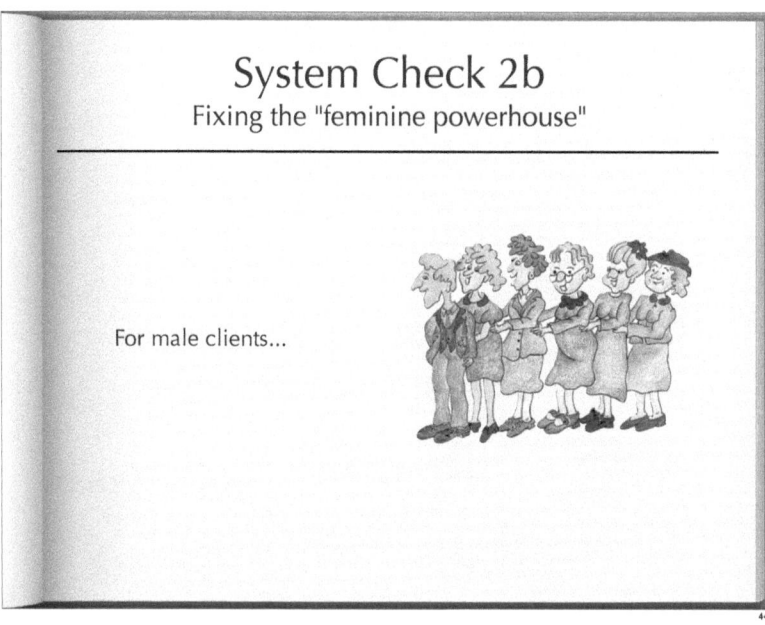

44

System Check 3
Correct internal picture of the family of origin

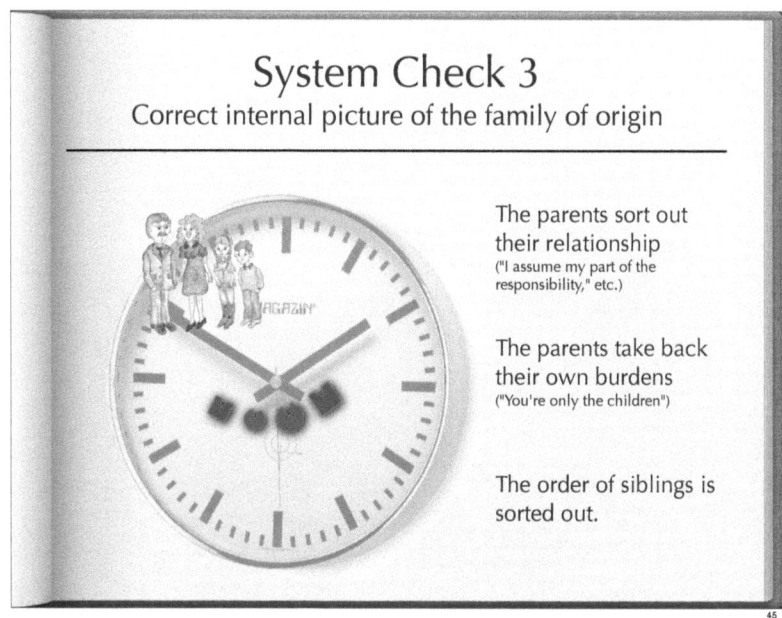

The parents sort out
their relationship
("I assume my part of the
responsibility," etc.)

The parents take back
their own burdens
("You're only the children")

The order of siblings is
sorted out.

45

System Check 4
A new system is established

The child separates from the family of origin
("Please look kindly on me as I go my way with ...")

The parents remain the parents
("Mom, Dad, my wife/my husband isn't taking anything away from you. You will always be my parents")

The partner may not take on the role of a parent
("I can now differentiate between you easily")

46

System Check 5
How did the chosen family form?

How did the parents get along before they had children?

How was it when the first child was born?

Let the family form step by step and always check how everyone feels.

47

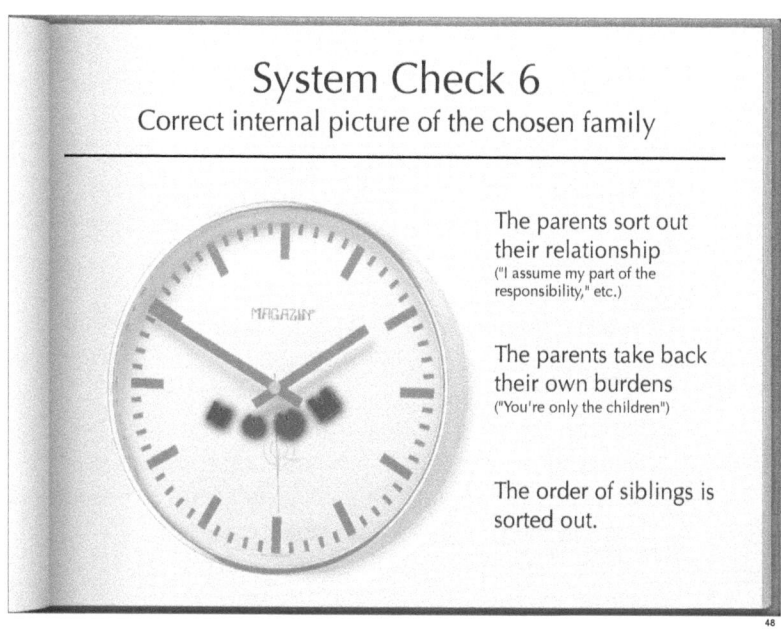

System Check 6
Correct internal picture of the chosen family

The parents sort out
their relationship
("I assume my part of the
responsibility," etc.)

The parents take back
their own burdens
("You're only the children")

The order of siblings is
sorted out.

48

9

Miscellaneous

49

What is systemically effective?

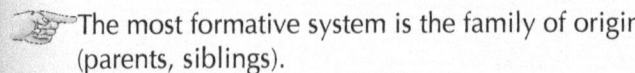 The most formative system is the family of origin (parents, siblings).

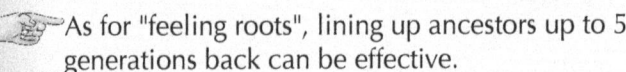 As for "feeling roots", lining up ancestors up to 5 generations back can be effective.

☞ In the chosen family (partner, children) entanglements in the family of origin frequently repeat, if the entanglements aren't resolved as far as the internal picture is concerned.

50

Does every problem
have a systemic cause?

Past
Lives

Conception   Birth   Present

karmic

Ancestors   **traumatic**

                        systemic-
                        traumatic

systemic

51

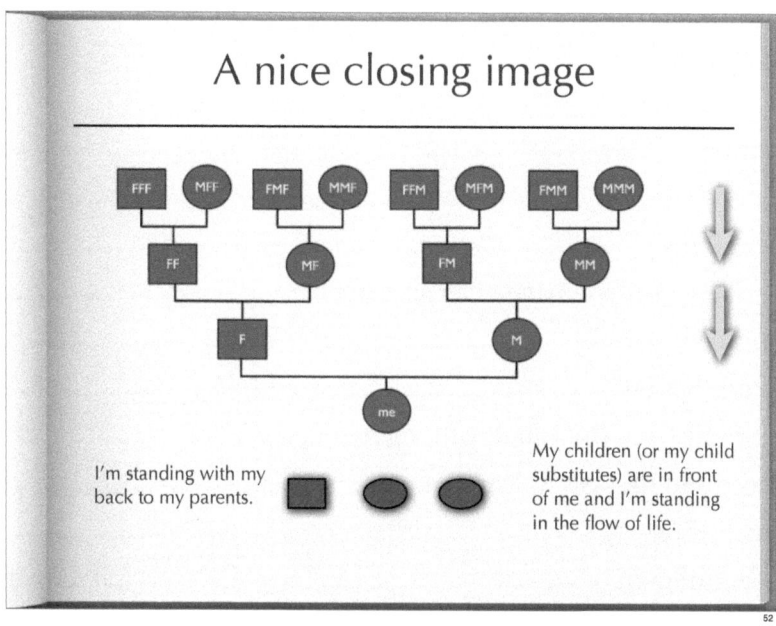

Index

Bibliography

Instead of a bibliography I appeal to your intuition as to picking the "right" books out of a huge selection on family and systemic therapy.

If you want a broad overview of constellation work, my favorite book in English is *"Family Constellations Revealed"* by Indra Torsten Preiss. While I stand apart from his guru Bert Hellinger who in my opinion treats his clients in a misanthropic fashion, Preiss delivers an easily understandable overview of what family constellation work can do when applied by a caring therapist.